DE SI RE

THE
SHAPE
OF
THINGS
TO
COME

gestalten

ABOUT DESIRE

The first decade of the 21st century already seems almost history. Perhaps we are now already experiencing something like the only appropriate moment to reflect on what was, what is, what is to come. Any look back at this point at the few years since the turn of the century is inevitably also a look forward to which of the countless major and minor episodes from the past few years has let behind something of substance, and this is what is needed to design the future.

One thing can be stated at the outset: if the 20th century was called the design century, this applies only to the industrial period of design, a time when the discipline was al-

lotted almost exclusively to the industrial production process, and when it shaped the design of an epoch, in symbiotic solidarity. This time has gone for good. Even though China, for example, can be considered the new home of world production, absolutely nothing is happening there that is repeating the emergence of Western industrial design. On the contrary, it is a Postmodern, almost surreal scenario that we are observing from a distance, a scenario that has elevated the simultaneity of a whole variety of epochs – agrarian society, early capitalism, Communism, industrial society, information society – into a principle, but a principle that is still unable to find an appropriate, that is to say independent, expressive design form for itself.

"IT IS THE PERVADING LAW OF ALL THINGS ORGANIC AND INORGANIC, OF ALL THINGS PHYSICAL AND METAPHYSICAL, OF ALL THINGS HUMAN AND ALL THINGS SUPER-HUMAN, OF ALL TRUE MANIFESTATIONS OF THE HEAD, OF THE HEART, OF THE SOUL, THAT THE LIFE IS RECOGNIZABLE IN ITS EXPRESSION, THAT FORM EVER FOLLOWS FUNCTION." Louis Henri Sullivan

On the other hand, the design concept that we are finding in this still young century has largely liberated itself from the clutches of industrial production. The "production trap", which classified every 20th century design in terms of its feasibility and economic viability, no longer clicks shut. Push processing, which states that supply drives markets, has not worked for a long time. And yet the 21st century is a design century as well – possibly to a much greater and more complex extent than the 20th century ever was. The number of names and styles that have placed themselves in the public eye in recent years is evidence of the immense power that design exercises over commerce and society. A power legitimised by the discipline's ability to give needs a visible form and to hand Postmodern man a screen onto which his desires, emotions and expectations can be projected. And we are not talking about basic needs here. These disappeared with the industrial age and the push market. No, we are talking about elaborate Postmodern needs: the need for individuality and differentiation, for beauty and insight, for pleasure and spirituality. However contradictory and diverse the scale of these needs might be, the more it provides a true image of modern consumer attitudes: the same person really can develop all these needs at the same time.

These hybrid needs are reflected in design, and vice versa: for example, design can be expressed in craft today without triggering an argument about whether such a combination is justified. Design can be expressed by harnessing complex technologies to its needs. Design can still be part of an industrial world or appropriate the mechanisms of the art market for itself. All that matters is to recognise that the design process is shaped by individuals and must work for individuals. Louis Henri Sullivan, who wrote the words that shaped industrial Modernism's view of design "form follows function", summed it all up over 110 years ago when he came up with the following formulation in his article "The Tall Building Artistically Considered" in Lippincott's Magazine: "It is the pervading law of all things organic and inorganic, of all things physical and metaphysical, of all things human and all things super-human, of all true manifestations of the head, of the heart, of the soul, that the life is recognizable in its expression, that form ever follows function."

It was opportune in the 20th century to allow form to follow function and to address technical function alone when considering function at all. Shortening Sullivan's thesis to the mere statement "form follows function" made the design process of the industrial age meaningful. In our century, it makes considerably more sense to read and understand Sullivan's thesis in full: all true manifestations of the head, the heart and the soul have their function, and thus of course also a form, that expresses them appropriately.

Desire, as a very human feeling, as a manifestation of the heart and the soul, is the key to this book. It intends to show how product design has developed since the turn of the century and to describe its new contexts so that they can be understood.

It is a book about the many possibilities that are open to design today and perhaps this also includes the possibility of a better future that is one of the discipline's age-old themes. A future that can be designed, in which individuals and their needs are taken seriously and expressed in everyday objects. Desire offers a survey of current product and interior design, a way of assessing what is new and what may gain a foothold, at least in the near future. Desire is a promise, and we are speculating about its redemption.

DESIGNING DESIRE

THE FACT IS THAT IT IS VERY DIFFICULT TO ARGUE THAT THERE IS ANY REAL PURPOSE IN THE DESIGN OF A CHAIR, WHICH A BRIEFING HAS LAID DOWN SHOULD BE LIKE ANY OTHER CHAIR, BUT DIFFERENT FROM IT.

Economic development, and the fact that the economy of basic needs has been transformed into an economy of desire, means that a process of profound transformation has begun for design as well. The reference system that shaped design in the 20th century has started to falter because of the dwindling importance of industrial production in Western societies and the associated increasing segmentation of markets. There are still areas in which design continues to play an integral role within an industrially determined process. But something else is true of the overwhelming number of areas, above all those that can be summed up primarily under the heading of consumer goods: the discipline that was shaped by the idea of functionalism until the 1980s found and still finds it difficult to come to terms with the apparently unavoidable development that probably started with the Memphis movement, and which is now the key factor in most areas, namely that of seeing design as mere formalism.

But this is precisely what it is all about. While in the last century design sought to define itself as a discipline above all by rendering itself distinct from art, it has recently lost this defining opposite. On the contrary, the former opposites, design and art, have moved towards each other in recent years, and largely follow the same rules in production and within market mechanisms. This applies whether it is achieving unique results by experimenting with materials, forms and processes, or in the system of marketing via galleries, trade fairs and auctions. If it is possible to define the essence of art as research for no specific purpose using artistic resources, then this definition can equally be applied to design. The fact is that it is very difficult to argue that there is any real purpose in the design of a chair, which a briefing has laid down should be like any other chair, but different from it, at least within the original definition of the purpose of industrial design. Well over ninety percent of all contemporary design work does not serve the idea of creating something radically new. Well over ninety percent of all design work is about competition differentiation within an existing product topology. It is about product differentiation, i.e. about modifying a familiar product and its typology, in order to design it more attractively for a defined target group.

The idea of product differentiation involves differentiation from the competitor's product as well as differentiation for the product range within one's own company. This is an all-embracing urge to differentiate that is one of the core theses of the economy of desire and all its pluralistic manifestations. Product differentiation defines differences in product quality between various products, and also differentiation of products that are the same and fulfil no technical function, but can satisfy different psychological or physical needs.

Design does still use industrial methods in product differentiation, but it has considerably changed its attitude to this. Until a few years ago, materials and technologies still actually determined the design of a product and also – and this is important for the development of the discipline – determined it ideologically, but now circumstances have changed to produce precisely the opposite. The design borrows a possible appearance that can be achieved through a manufacturing method or a particular material, in order to transform it into a different context. The consequence is that in furniture or car manufacturing, for example, there are scarcely any purely industrial processes, but craft activities are always included in order to achieve the desired result after a tangible product differentiation. The designer wants to achieve a particular look for his product, and on the basis of his now artistic and entrepreneurial responsibility becomes a researcher, looking for an appropriate way of implementing his ideas. The effect he achieves in the best case: the person looking at the completed work is amazed, and asks: "How can this be possible?"

But this approach in the design process is made possible above all because of the change in general economic conditions. Companies are no longer concerned with market shares, or with producing as much as possible as cheaply as possible. They are about enhancing productivity, i.e. the quality of the production. If a product looks to be of higher quality, and the look can be new or simply different, but must seem to represent high calibre, then there is a chance of creating goods to meet consumers' ever more sophisticated needs for items to consume.

Design, which has liberated itself from industrial conditions and the associated physical demands on the dimensions of what can be made, can take on any form. The question about the appropriate form for an object, which should arise from its function, has become redundant, since thousands of functions can be stored on media that are only a few nanometres in size.

Beyond this, there are no patterns of behaviour or rules for designers any more that draw on an ideology with discipline inherent in it. They are able to decide individually on the approach taken by their work and the way they act as market participants. They can cling on to the old idea of design that is able to change and improve people's everyday culture. They can see themselves as exploring new forms and construction principles, or conceive their frame of reference in the context of ecological questions. But they can also simply pursue the idea of becoming rich and famous, without being tormented by pangs of conscience, as they would have been in past views of design.

Despite all the artistic freedom offered by the economics of desire, they find themselves within a hard-fought competition of identities. They have to develop an identifiable handwriting that is theirs and theirs alone. As well as working for other people, for companies, they have to pursue their own projects and communicate their meaning, so that like artists they make their position clear to the public. The good thing about this is that the approach that produces a design can be a quite different one the next day. Just as consumers treat consumption dialectically, designers can behave dialectically as well. They can work on a whole variety of projects at the same time, plunging into different stylistic worlds in order to lend form to their desires.

But 21st century design is individualists' design to only a limited extent. Design still acts within a stylistic system that is pluralistic in a way that it was not in times of functionalism, and that is essentially characterised by four questions that certainly do imply aesthetic expression and a design language: can Modernism be continued? What does the future look like? How can I entertain you? What can I contribute to creating or sustaining an environment that is worth living in? On the one hand these are conservative and liberal, hedonistic and social questions, and on the other they are questions that are directed at popular or elitist themes, at innovative or traditional concepts. They are starting points for formulating group-specific replies. And in these replies they find different, but identifiable aesthetic preferences. Here we are dealing with stylistic characteristics that permeate every design and can thus be located within a stylistic system. So these design languages behave like aesthetic models or visual expressions of social ideas that are taking place and extending themselves at the same time.

This survey of design at the end of the first decade of the 21st century uses a system of four identifiable aesthetic models, and has placed those involved in each together in groups that sum up the significance of the questions they are asking: modernists, inventor, tale-tellers, entertainers. This form of categorisation is intended to consider current design developments in the context of the way in which they emerge, and to find patterns to explain what themes are being acted out by the different designer personalities, why a design looks like this and nothing else, and – presumably much more importantly – why and for whom this design represents an object of desire. For there is one thing we should not forget: in the 2.0 economy of desires, designers have taken on the role of advisers and chairpersons who place their skills at the service individuals and mediate between their requirements and those of the market.

THE ECONOMY OF DESIRE

THE MARKET IS NO LONGER CHARACTERISED BY A GROUP, BUT DEFINED BY EACH INDIVIDUAL WITH HIS OR HER SPECIFIC NEEDS.

Various explanations are given for why the Italian designers Ettore Sottsass, Michele De Lucchi and Matteo Thun founded the Memphis movement around the turn of the year 1980/81. One widely-held view sees Memphis as a critique of the principles of functionalism that had dominated design since the late 1960s. Another view sees Memphis merely as a parallel development in design to Postmodern architecture, which was promoting a similar formal language in another dimension at the same time.

But there are also attempts to interpret the Memphis movement as located above all in a social dimension. One of these looks at the situation of designers who increasingly, because of their dependence on an industrial system, felt they were no longer able to see themselves as being able to use their work to improve people's everyday lives, and as a response to this developed a design language made up of individual artistic impulses. Another interpretation looks at the dimen-

sion of how design was generally perceived at this time. Ettore Sottsass and Michele De Lucchi were said to have been infected with the idea of making design objects accessible to the masses as well, in other words with democratising design via a popular, i.e. above all spectacular mode of appearance.

But how could the formal, at a first glance arbitrary accumulation of basic geometrical solids (cones, spheres, pyramids or cubes), usually in primary colours, lead to the enormous popularity that Memphis achieved in an incredibly short time, not only in the Western world but also in shaping the way design is understood in general, right down to the present day?

Memphis seemed to focus on a type of consumer that had not existed before. This was the need to see everyday items as a medium for expressing one's own identity by using products. Memphis was not like anything that had been available to buy before. Memphis was anti-design, it contradicted every current view of industrial design, which always seemed to start from the point of analysing what was technically and commercially feasible. Until Memphis, the appearance of industrial society had hitherto been reduced to the principle of the (process-related) remoulding of forms, as a consequence of arguments about functionalism.

The Memphis movement did away with this adherence to rules. The erosion process for mass markets, which had already begun in the late 60s, caused different consumer needs to germinate in Western societies for the first time. The general mass market, in which push processing, i.e. supply that dictated demand, quickly became history. A new economy emerged from the economy of basic needs, which aimed at supplying people with essentials and tried to provide this supply almost as a monopoly, on the basis of a kind of welfare idea. This new economy was shaped by demand on the consumer side. Consumers had gained in self-confidence. They developed their own ideas about creating a context for their lives. They started to have concrete ideas and wishes. The economy of desire came into being.

This economy is characterised by a wide-ranging segmentation of markets, caused by increasingly sophisticated consumer needs in relation to the product worlds that surround them. In the initial phase of the economy of desire these are still needs that grow out of a particular group dynamic. In other words, it is still relatively easy for a supplier of products to identify needs, bundle them and direct what they are able to supply at these needs, as consumers within a particular group usually behave homogeneously. When the Memphis movement popularised the design concept in the 1980s, in many fields it was enough simply to use the designation "designer product" to command a higher price than was possible without that designation. For the first time, higher value can be created by formal differentiation in cases of interchangeable product quality and performance. As a consequence, design loses the reference system of post-war Modernism – technical function, industrial production, mass market – and at the same time gains a new one: communication becomes design's new central function

and replaces the product performance of an industrial nature, which is directed at technical function. Design now communicates an aesthetic experience. Design makes it possible for users to identify with fairly specific values and attitudes to life. For example, this can apply to projecting social status or a particular lifestyle.

For industry, increasing productivity against the background of an increasingly segmented market structure becomes a central challenge. The idea is – in global competition as well – to reduce production costs and at the same time raise the quality of the resulting products, and thus increase productivity. Since the 1990s, industry has increasingly seen design as an instrument for differentiating product ranges that can successfully make emotional contact with segments of the market that are becoming ever smaller.

But in the globalisation years, the intensity of competition has constantly increased. More and more market participants are fighting for the favours of a consumer who is now no longer part of a homogeneous group, as at the beginning of the economy of desire, but who takes the liberty of consuming in one way today and in exactly the opposite way tomorrow. In segmented markets, brands become more important for consumers as identifying patterns that make it possible for people to make themselves distinct from other groups, or show their allegiance to certain ones. But alongside the desire to belong to a group and to use products to symbolise this, there is a desire within the group for individual consumption. And this dialectic of consumer behaviour has led to the formation of a new, inevitable and weird target group: hybrid consumers.

So mere differentiation of product ranges via a specific design leads in a second phase to the individualisation of products. Mobile phone cover, accessories for products such as the iPod or the car configurators offered by most manufacturers are examples of how users can tailor products ranges to their own specific needs through defined or open kit systems.

More and more branches are exploring a new form of production today: mass customisation. This involves individualised mass production focused on individual customer wishes and the greatest possible flexibility. But of course only products made up of various individual parts are suitable for mass customisation. Another problem for mass customisation is that knowledge of consumer needs will inevitably always be restricted: this is not about target groups with the same characteristics, but about particular individuals.

In principle, a company must have every conceivable individual part read for every conceivable combination, in order to be able to respond appropriately to individual wishes.

Thus it is only logical and consistent to develop ideas of individualisation further in the direction of making personalised products available. In future, it will become necessary to develop a single product for a customer, a unique object tailored to its users' body like a bespoke suit. The fact is that there has now been a 2.0 economy of desire for a long time. The internet has influenced every sphere of our lives, and changes the economy and society at a speed that would have seemed utopian even a few years ago.

But unlike the New Economy of the turn of the millennium, which is above all based on visions, the Web 2.0 is an extremely real thing, and its is also changing the economy of desire. Seen in perspective, the market is no longer characterised by a group, but defined by each individual with his or her specific needs. The consumer becomes the market participant. The very possibility of being able to communicate oneself to others becomes more important than the content of what is communicated: in isolation, each market participant seeks a form of exchange with others that is not directed at fulfilling a particular consumer wish, but at interaction as a consumer experience in its own right. Phenomena such a blogs, YouTube, Facebook or the Second Life are interaction platforms, and they make an enormous impact on companies' product development. The Open Source technology developed for the internet, which means that users can help to write programme content, can also be seen as a strategy for integrating consumers into processes that are relevant to commerce, such as the product development of consumer goods. In the world of Open Source design, consumers take on the role of co-designers, as active market participants. They influence the design to the extent of defining their personal requirements – physical, technological, aesthetic. This means that in fact personalised products are emerging for the first time that are not made by craft processes such as bespoke tailoring, for example, but take over new technologies. New processes for endowing with form – like stereo lithography or 3D printing – now used essentially for producing prototypes, can also be considered for producing "personal design" as technologies of the future.

Industrial production will continue to wane in significance. The fact is that industrial production can scarcely still be located in the globalised economy of desire. The search for ever cheaper production sites worldwide may help an enterprise to make higher profits in the short term. But even now, the sub-contractor principle tends to predominate. A sub-contractor contracted to produce goods commissions a sub-contractor who commissions a sub-contractor to produce etc. So more and more firms no longer know who actually makes their products. This means that in the long term they lose one of their most important arguments in the global battle for customers: source, credibility, authenticity.

Given the continuing technical revolution, we are constantly faced with new challenges. But not only that: design will also have to manage the increasing complexity of a world of many divergent consumer needs. Because even in the 2.0 economy of desire the human being remains the measure of discipline.

Andrej Kupetz

··

THE MODERNISTS

IDEALISM / FORMALISM / CLASSICISM / BRAINSCRIPT / LIMITED EDITIONS / CONSTRUCTIVISM / SUPER NORMAL / ECLECTICISM / MEMORABLE ICONS

··

ADRIEN ROVERO / ALAIN GILLES / ALEXANDER LERVIK / AUTOBAN / BARBER OSGERBY / BLESS / CENTRALA / CHRISTOPHE DELCOURT / D.E. SELLERS / DAVE KEUNE / DIRK WINKEL / DUSTDE-LUXE / EVA MARGUERRE / FABIEN CAPPELLO / FORMFJORD / FORM US WITH LOVE / FOR USE / FREDRIK MATTSON / FRONT / FURNITURE FOR DAILY USE / GEOFFREY LILGE / GUILLAUME DELVIGNE / HANNES WETTSTEIN / HERME CISCAR & MÓNICA GARCÍA / IONNA VAUTRIN / JASPER MORRISON / JUNIO DESIGN / KURSI / LIFEGOODS / MARK BRAUN / MATTHEW HILTON / MICHAEL BIHAIN / MICHAEL YOUNG / MIKIYA KOBAYASHI / MIKKO LAAKKONEN / NAOKI HIRAKOSO / MIN CHEN / NEO DESIGN / O-D-A / OSKO+DEICHMANN / PATRICK GAVIN / PATRICK NORGUET / PATRICIA URQUIOLA / PETER BRANDT / PHILIP EDIS / RAINER SPEHL / RAPHAËL VON ALLMEN / RONAN & ERWAN BOUROULLEC / STEFAN BORSELIUS / STUDIO GORM / STUDIOILSE / STUDIO LO / TAF / TAKASHI SATO / TAKESHI MIYAKAWA / TOM DIXON / ÜNAL & BÖLER STUDIO / VIABLE LONDON / VOONWONG&BENSONSAW

··

MODERNISTS ARE FIRST AND FOREMOST IDEALISTS. THE PROBLEM THEY SHARE WITH MANY IDEALISTS FROM OTHER DISCIPLINES IS THAT THEIR IDEALS ARE OUT OF DATE.

Modernists live in the past, and cannot or will not see that Modernism has come to an end because of the changed economic, social and technological situation. Unmoved by this, they have given themselves over in their work to a kind of formalism that celebrates and repeats the formal language of Modernism, develops it further and applies it to product typologies that still did not exist at the time of Modernism. Jonathan Ives's work for Apple, for example, essentially quotes the designer Dieter Rams, whom he reveres, who shaped the image of Braun in the 1950s and 60s. It is just that in Rams' day there were no iPods or laptops.

One of the most remarkable works presented at the 2008 Milan Furniture Fair was JASPER MORRISON'S Basel Chair for Vitra. At a first glance, Basel is a classic product of the industrial age, strongly reminiscent of the 1935 Frankfurt Chair attributed to Max Stoelcker. Its form has been seen so often that it seems as familiar to us as if it had always been around. A brain script opens up in our minds and memories are awakened.

Jasper Morrison Basel Chair

A chair of the kind that would have been justified in appearing in any public place in the 20th century, in cafés, schools, at socialist party conferences or in community centres. Basel is the public chair. Jasper Morrison borrowed the design, but he interprets it in a spirit of Modernism: by changing the material quality – he uses an extremely thin-walled plastic for the seats – he manages to lend an aesthetic quality to this banal wooden chair, the epitome of public seating. In this way, he improves things that cannot be improved. He transforms Modernism into the formalism of Postmodernism, an essential feature of the Modernist's work.

Jasper Morrison has already accumulated some experience in this field. Even two years earlier, in 2006, he delivered what was undoubtedly the big hit of the entire Milan Fair, without the design being shown there at all. It was a simple crate, put together from a few planks. The crate measures 50 cm x 17.5 cm x 37.5 cm, is made of Norwegian Douglas fir

and manufactured in Great Britain, so "British made", as the producer Established & Sons, owned by Stella McCartney's husband Alasdair Willis stresses, and which is expressed in the crate's proud prize. It may be surprising that anything at all is still produced in post-industrial Great Britain – above all when a wine box is taken into consideration, because that is precisely what Jasper Morrison has redesigned in the form of The Crate. But what prompted Jasper Morrison of all people, the British designer who sees his work as a continuation of Modernism's design ideas in an industrial context, to deliver something that is essentially coarse craftsmanship, which caused the Boston Globe to ask: "Why spend $171 on an ersatz wine box when you can use a real one for free?" Wine boxes, says Morrison, have served him so well in his Paris home as a way of storing books and magazines that he could not see the point of trying to invent anything better.

That is certainly true, and it is possible to understand it if the crate is placed in the context of an exhibition project, which is what Morrison did in the same year, working with the Japanese designer Naoto Fukasawa in Tokyo. Using the title Super Normal, the designers brought everyday utility objects together that only earn a place in life because they are useful. They are so conspicuously to be taken for granted that they simply seem supernormal to us. Morrison and Fukasawa are celebrating this fact of being taken for granted in their exhibition, and turning against design that is useless and intended only to attract attention.

So the argument about useful and useless design has found new and fertile soil again, and new figures to involve themselves in it. It could be that The Crate marked the beginning of a new minimalism, but one that could have come about only because of the frenzy for decoration that had possessed people in recent years, without really giving the discipline anything new. For it has to be said that this is now all looking a little tired. At best The Crate attracted attention. And one thing is certain: The Crate is first and foremost anti-design, owing more to art than to anything else.

Jasper Morrison's co-curator Naoto Fukasawa has been something like a Far Eastern disciple of the Modernists ever since his pioneering design of a CD player for Muji. In the midst of complete general intoxication with multi-functionalism, Fukasawa designed a CD player that can only play CDs and nothing else, except that it hangs on the wall like a cuckoo clock. And his design in its turn quotes the formal language of Braun's 1960s appliances with its typical dot grids. The player is switched on and off by a cord of the kind we are familiar with from ancient standard lamps. The sound quality produced by this first mono player for 40 years is lousy, but that is not what it is about either. Fukasawa is a man who is applying the brakes, a simplifier. All his designs – whether they are furniture (e.g. for B&B), lamps (Nadja Swarowski), consumer electrical appliances (Muji) or mobile phones (LG) – are driven by craft detailing that has something incredibly out of date about it, but it is evidence of a profoundly felt humanism. Fukasawa's work could be seen as a refusal to accept the technologisation of our environment, or as a philosophical achievement in attaining a human scale.

But Modernists are lining up on the old continent as well. The Bouroullec brothers from France, for example, have developed into genuine exponents of stylistics. Even though the **BOUROULLECS** have been making their mark on international design events for some years, they can still be counted among the most important newcomers because they are so young. The Bourroulec phenomenon is exciting for two reasons: they made their name through the art market, i.e. through gallery launches (Galerie Kreo Paris) of their prototypes. But, unlike Ron Arad, for example, or Marc Newson, who use sculptor's materials such as steel and

Ronan & Erwan Bouroullecs
Kreo Gallery Exhibition, Blacklight

marble for their design work, the Bourroullec brothers have addressed all aspects of the cheap industrial material plastic, and implement the basic idea of industrial design, serial production, in a fascinating way that is reminiscent of Jacques Tati's films. Somehow or other, their designs always seem old-fashioned, and it is precisely this that lends them an almost magical charm. Their Papyrus Chair for Kartell, introduced in Milan in 2008 is – like all other Kartell products – made of polycarbonate, and its form makes viewers

think of Modernist fibre-glass reinforced shell chairs at the same time, but there has never been any such thing in the translucent aesthetic of polycarbonate. The Bourroullecs' designs are never without irony, just as if they had come into being in conflict with today's knowledge and the belief in the future that prevailed in the 1950s. The second reason: there are scarcely any other designers today who are models for the new designer generation to the same extent. Soulmates of the Bourroullecs can be found at degree shows anywhere between London, Berlin and Lausanne.

And that is precisely where **RAPHAEL VON ALLMEN** comes from. This young Swiss designer showed an aluminium chair with a removable plastic seat at imm cologne. This seat can only be shifted into the third dimension by being cut to size under tension. The Bourroullecs conducted a similar experiment in the previous year with their Stealwood chair for Magis, which they have complemented this year with an office furniture programme (consisting of shelf and table systems). But von Allmen's chair – in the spirit of the Modernists' idea – is more logical than the Bourroullec

ECAL/Raphael von Allmen
Plastic Back Chair

design, which has to work with semi-finished products to achieve its desired effect in combining contrasting materials such as wood and metal.

Or take the young Berlin designer **MARK BRAUN**, with his Lingor ceiling lamp series, also launched in Cologne, which was produced in phosphorescent enamelled sheet steel using a traditional pressed metal process. These lamps combine traditional technology and industrial-looking design, which feels both familiar and at the same time new to us. The Bourroullecs achieved a similar effect with their Bell lamps, which they have shown since 2005 in various small series at the Galerie Kreo in Paris. These oversized, black bell-shaped lamps borrow their design language from our ideas of

Mark Braun Lingor

· ·

industrial Modernism, but make them look unduly sensual on grounds of their sheer size alone.

The **BARBER OSGERBY** practise operates in London, and they were once called the new Modernists by the internet magazine Metropolis. And that is quite right: the members of the BarberOsgerby practise have mastered the art of shifting banal forms into different contexts. Their current "Delta Tables" series for Established & Sons is reminiscent in its formal language of melamine – the most beloved plastic in the 1960s. For their "Bottle table" for Cappellini (2007) they used an enlarged bottle shape in marble as the foot for a round marble tabletop. BarberOsgerby also seem to be interested in their new designs in accumulating or stacking geometrical solids, as demonstrated by the Memphis movement over twenty-five years

BarberOsgerby Saturn Stool

ago. For example, they developed the Cupola glass object for Meta, combining hand-blown glass with marble and metal and piling the individual solids on top of each other like a pyramid. Here they are quoting Ettore Sottsass's work in the early 1980s for the Murano glass industry in the Veneto, which was short of ideas at the time, and so – whether consciously or unconsciously – introduced a kind of Memphis Design revival.

At least this proved that the Modernists represent a Postmodernist movement, and are not so much rooted in Modernism as in the here and now. This fact is underlined by **TOM DIXON'S** work. Dixon is a self-taught designer who would actually have preferred to be a musician. He came to furniture design in the late 1980s more or less by chance, developed some incredibly exciting seating sculptures in the 1990s, and then started a commercial career as art director of Habitat. Now his Tom Dixon collection has extended into a full range, and he has created a world that almost perfectly imi-

Tom Dixon Mirror Balls on Stand

tates Modernism between the 1940s in America and Italy in the 1970s, if it were not for recurrent surprises in the form of games with the dimensions of the products and unusual typologies, for example the Copper Shade or Mirror Ball lamp clusters. Ultimately they make the Tom Dixon collection very up to date – following the motto "something good from earlier to make something pleasant today".

The designers from the Turkish **AUTOBAN** practise, founded in 2003 in Istanbul, also consciously play with the materials and formal language of classical Modernism in their work. Wooden stools using ancient forms are reminiscent of the work of Ray and Charles Eames, and organically shaped marble tables remind us of Eero Saarinen's designs for Knoll; geometrical sofa bodies float on graceful feet as they used to for Ludwig Mies van der Rohe. Even if when looking at the Autoban furniture we are tempted to call

Autoban Booklamp

up one brainscript after another, it is never quite possible to do this successfully. The objects constantly look new and up-to-date.

This is also precisely what happens to us with the Apple products mentioned earlier: the design language of Modernism can be transferred into the Postmodern world, and it suits that world extremely well.

1 Taste of Tea armchair
What distinguishes an armchair from a chair? The armrests. This one is composed of two parts, frame and seat, generating the armrests through the structure itself while giving the legs an oblique symmetry.

2 NRML chair
Simple straight lines were the starting point for this re-interpretation of the common chair. Selecting an unusually canted position for the rear legs, O-D-A nonetheless provided a comfortably angled backrest on an opposing diagonal to create a stackable chair.

1

2

NAOKI HIRAKOSO
3 Slitta lounge chair
4 Slitta lounge chair and ottoman
Slitta is a lounge chair designed with simple lines, with the form based on research on the human form and its lines. Even though the structure has no cushioning, it is slightly bent by body weight when sat on, thus affording a comfortable sitting posture that is not too stiff, and not too easy.

3

4

MICHAEL YOUNG
1 Coen chair

HERME CISCAR & MÓNICA GARCÍA
2 Scala chair

MIKIYA KOBAYASHI
3 Cielo armchair
4 Brio easy chair
An eclectic mix of materials creates familiar objects: the Brio easy chair and Cielo armchair are both framed in unusual shades of tubular steel mixed with fabric upholstery and caned rattan. Sustainable rattan regrows within five to 10 years, as opposed to the 50 to 70 years taken by wood.

1

2

3

4

TOM DIXON
Slab table and chairs with Beat lights
The Slab collection is made from specially crowned oak and is characterised by a deeply brushed and heavily lacquered surface. The Beat lights were inspired by the water-carrying vessels still in widespread use in India. Made from hand-beaten brass, they also borrowed the rapidly vanishing skills of Indian master craftsmen for their production.

MATTHEW HILTON
1 Fin dining chair
2 Light Oval table
3 Colombo chair

CHRISTOPHE DELCOURT OBJETS /MOBILIER
Christophe Delcourt
4 OVO
Its four legs rendered in black waxed steel,
Ovo's tabletop is made in tinted oak.

ÜNAL & BÖLER STUDIO
Alper Böler, Ömer Ünal, Meral Göktekin
5 Kase
Kase ("bowl" in Turkish) uses a centrally
anchored set of nesting metal bowls to
create a coffee table that holds magazines
and newspapers upright like the petals of
a particularly graphical flower.

1

3

2

4

5

19

1 One Armed chair
Breaking convention, this chair features four legs but only one arm. Its asymmetry recalls a school desk with writing tablet. When two are set side-by-side (with arms on the outside) they can also form a bench.

2 Sledge lounge chair
Signature for Autoban, this generously proportioned lounge chair draws inspiration from childhood memories. Sledge reminded its designers of playing outdoors on snowy winter days, while actually providing cosy refuge inside.

3 Sleepy rocking chair
Sleepy is not your grandmother's rocking chair. Its legs and arms are manufactured as a single element while the seat and backrest can be upholstered in fabric or leather.

4 Kahve chair
Taking inspiration from typical Turkish coffeehouse chairs, Kahve is a marriage of tradition and contemporary design. With the legs and back panel developed as a one-piece unit, it also conveys technical innovation.

5 Booklamp
Is it a lamp? Is it a bedside table? It's both. Booklamp both illuminates and provides storage for night-time reading.

6 Starfish table
A table that features legs inspired by the sea creature.

7 Scrub table
A functional table is made whimsical with legs that appear to have been uprooted from the garden.

AUTOBAN
Seyhan Özdemir & Sefer Çağlar
Pages 12,15, 20–21, 44

Most often the work of Istanbul-based Autoban is a celebration of the emotional power of everyday objects made new. The legs of the Scrub table look as if they've been pulled up from garden soil while the upholstered Kahve is an updated version of the traditional Turkish coffeehouse chair, with legs and backrest manufactured as a single unit.

Architect Seyhan Özdemir and interior designer Sefer Çağlar met at Mimar Sinan Fine Arts University, graduating in 1998 and establishing Autoban five years later. They quickly became known for their design of Istanbul's House Café chain; a series of boutiques for fashion label, Vakko; and the warmly wooden Muze de Changa restaurant. The studio's critically acclaimed product design actually came out of their interiors work, as the couple searched for but were unable to find the right pieces to compliment their domestic and residential projects.

In 2008, Spanish furniture retailer De La Espada began to produce and globally distribute selected Autoban pieces under the label Autoban Built by De La Espada, considerably invigorating its inventory and broadening its market. Taken as a whole, the studio's work is a union of contradictions usually producing powerful forms and emotive environments: they unite metal (aluminum, brass, iron) and wood, and combine shapes that then become, as the studio phrases it, "strongly simple": Pebble is an oak or walnut table with a softly rounded surface and brightly coloured legs made from plate iron. The oversized lounge chair (as if seen through a child's eyes) called Sledge was inspired by childhood memories. While providing a comfortable refuge inside, it becomes doubly comforting because its shape reminds one of playing outside on a wintry day. One thing is certain: Özdemir and Çağlar's nostalgia has helped to put Turkey on the map for modern design.

5

6

7

HALDANE MARTIN
Pages 22, 62, 173

Haldane Martin's work tends to make references to regional cultural history and evoke the emerging South African identity. The architecture and furniture design studio was formed in 2002 in Cape Town. The practise consists of nine designers under the aegis of Haldane Martin himself, who was born in Johannesburg in 1970 and earned his degree in industrial design in 1992.

Sometimes the office's work is also sustainable in its production and the materials used: his Zulu Mama café chair is made using recycled plastic woven into a bowl shape by rural women who are familiar with an indigenous Zulu basket weaving technique. The Fiela Feather lights look like huge white tulips made of feathers with a long, arcing metal stem. Made from lightly finished wood, the studio's New Slant shelving system consists of modular boxes that are attracted, and attached, to each other via magnets embedded in each shelf. The most unconventional of Martin's 25-piece furniture line, however, is the Songololo couch, a centipede-like redux of the 70s sectional by Ueli Berger inspired by "nature's creepy crawlies." Narrow modular cushion-leg panels can be added on or taken away to suit the size of the interior. A toy for adults or world-class deisgn? Both.

1   New Slant shelving system
    The slanted modular boxes of New Slant are attracted to each other via embedded magnets, allowing users to build a variety of configurations. Under the sponsorship of the Department of Arts and Culture, Martin was invited to Design Indaba, where he created the shelving as part of a sustainable job solution for the disabled workers of Carecraft who manufacture the design.

2   Weightless Tub chair
    An exercise in the ecological principal of maximum resource efficiency, this chair's lightweight recycled stainless steel frames and laminated plywood seats were inspired by the revolutionary Eames chairs of the 1940's and South African wirework sculptures.

3   Zulu Mama chair
    Zulu Mama are made using an indigenous Zulu basket-weaving technique adapted for recycled plastic. Work generated in the service of the weaving contributes to the economic empowerment of rural women.

4   Simplicity Chaise
    Originally designed for use in a wellness spa, Simplicity's form and proportions have a calming quality. The use of inguni hide identifies the piece as luxuriously African.

5   Fiela Feather Arc light
    Fiela is named after Dalene Mathews' book "Fiela se Kind," set in Oudtshoorn, the same ostrich farming district from which the soft white feathers that form the spherical diffuser are sourced. The sustainable design uses energy-saving CFL lamps, recycled stainless steel frames and feathers that are a by-product of the ostrich hide industry.

6   Riempie dining chair
    The Riempie Chair was inspired by antique Cape Dutch furniture, the traditional leather thongs of which have been replaced with plastic in a Malaysian hand-caned pattern.

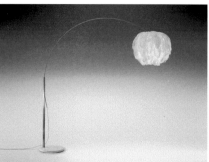

TOM DIXON

1   Cone light
Inspired by professional photographers'
equipment and domesticated for the
home, Cone light suits any environment.

2   Mirror Balls on stand
Inspired by the lunar landing space
helmets, this lamp is fashioned from
the same high-impact-resistant polycarbonate used in bullet-proofing and
anti-vandal applications, making it
almost indestructible.

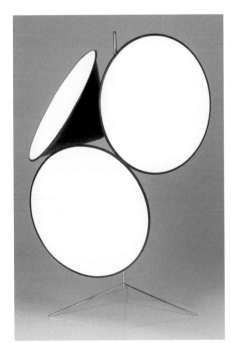

1

2

1

2

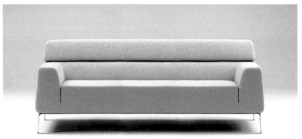

3

4

HANNES WETTSTEIN
Scope light
In 1980, Wettstein created the Snodo
task light for Belux which, 27 years later,
inspired this family of lights, for the same
company, called Scope. It exploits "Easy
Move", an invisible bal-ance mechanism
designed by Belux engineer Volker Richter
and features a large working radius.

Métis lounge chair
Wettstein's first project for Lapalma is a
lounge chair with three legs and a wide
seat in curved plywood (and other materials
better suited to outdoor use).

OSKO+DEICHMANN
Clip chair
Inspired by a small, fold-up basket found
by the designers in a Bulgarian market that
featured single slats beaded on ropes to
form two hinged surfaces that could
be transformed into a curved three dimensional object. Improving on this mechanism, the slats of this foldable lounge chair
form a comfortable seat and a sculptural
object when open or closed.

1

2

3

4

5

MICHAEL YOUNG
Pages 17, 27, 41

From sex toys that are easy on sensitive skin to the interiors of a plastic surgery clinic, from mouses and lighting to pet furniture, Michael Young's design is marked by its clean contours, exhilarating colour and, invisible to users, the hands-on investigation into and clever use of materials and manufacturing techniques. Born in Sunderland, England in 1966, Young graduated in furniture and product design at Kingston University in 1992 and then worked for four years at a design studio headed by Tom Dixon called Space. In 1995, Young established MY – 022 Ltd design office in London, working for clients such as Cappellini, Sawaya & Moroni, Galerie KREO and Pearl Lam's Contrasts Gallery. His Sticklight, like a large cocktail stirrer, for Eurolounge has become easily recognised, along with a dog house he created for Magis in 2001. Young moved shop to Iceland to focus more on design, and then to Hong Kong to be closer to manufacturers. Since then, his projects have included a bicycle for Giant, barware for Schweppes and new work for Established & Sons. For Accupunto in 2007, Young designed the hooded two-seat sofa called Sun Ra from Viro Fibre, as well as his softly curved teak Capra stool and Coen chair. Simultaneously playful and dead-serious about his work, Young has proven time and again that there isn't a design problem out there that he can't resolve.

Sun Ra sofa

FORMFJORD

1 Void coffee table
   The elegant frame of prototype low table Void makes soft folds from polished aluminum.

JETHRO MACEY

2 Textile credenza
   Inspired by Macey's concrete tiles, Textile applies the same strong aesthetic to a collection of side units, CNC-milled Corian doors, lacquered flanks and a solid wood base.

1

2

CHRISTOPHE DELCOURT OBJETS /MOBILIER
Christophe Delcourt

3 POL desk and ALP lamp
   POL is lacquered aluminium while the table lamp comes in lacquered steel.

DUSTDELUXE
Damien Gernay

4 Cramp table
   Cramp explores the representation of an object in a synthetic manner. The table is composed of multiple contrasting layers, from oak to epoxy resin. The sharp edges typical of wooden assemblies are softened in Cramp in order to offer the necessary curvaceous base for application of the resin.

3

4

PHILIP EDIS
Authority System storage
A storage system that takes its cue from the monolithic buildings that host institutions of authority, safe-keeping, surveillance and other protective organisations. The exterior looks brutalist and highly secure but elegant. Inside, the cabinet and chest of drawers are more inviting, with lighter colours and a softer shape.

Folkform seems not to look for pat answers but rather for enlightening questions. What happens, for instance, when you combine fakes with the real thing? Or, more specifically, what happens when you combine an original material with imitations? The Stockholm-based design collective was founded by industrial designers Chandra Ahlsell (1973) and Anna Holmquist (1978) in 2004. Within four years, the duo, already demonstrating a talent for materials investigation, had been nominated for the Swedish Design Award.

At the 2006 Salone Satellite, Folkform introduced Material Merge, which explored how to elevate a modest material such as hardboard Masonite. They mixed actual flowers and butterflies into the huge Masonite production presses to make an organic ornament that would be embedded permanently in the Masonite. A year later, a jury for Material Connexion voted it into the company's New York materials archive.

The Unique Standard collection revisited this theme, debuting during Stockholm Design Week in 2008. The Unique Standard group included Bench With Three Types of Leather, which combined imitation leather and the original leather from Danish designer Arne Jacobsen's Swan Chair in a daybed, mixing tufting and stitching patterns to strong effect. The studio's MDF and Granite Display Case and the Masonite Chest with 18 Drawers (Masonite hardboard grafted onto birch wood) are both pretty patchworks of material while the Marble Cabinet unites Carrara marble with a marble laminate. The questions are timely: does authenticity always determine value nowadays? Who decides whether an object is precious?

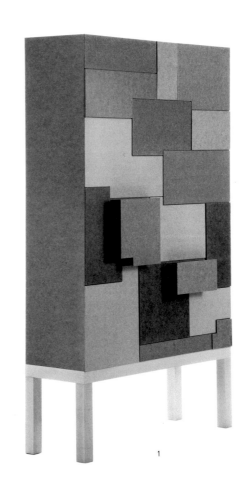

1

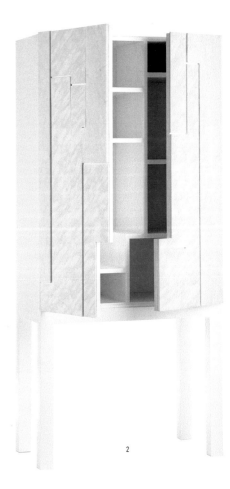

2

1 Masonite Chest with 18 drawers
2 Marble Cabinet
3 MDF and Granite Display Case
4 Bench with Three Types of Leather
   The Unique Standard collection offers new interpretations of today's most common materials while questioning our perception of and associations with them. What happens when an original or authentic material is combined with materials that mimic it?

4

3

1

RAINER SPEHL
1 Hanging Closet
Everything about Hanging is unexpected: it resembles a square, instead of a round tree trunk and hangs on the wall instead of standing on the floor.

2 The New Konk furniture
The furniture in this luminous retail interior offers both fantasy and a tiny journey of discovery: chicken bones hang in mobiles from the ceiling, a forest grows in the dressing room and crooked furniture suggests insects.

2

BLESS
Workingbed
A dual-purpose piece of furniture – bed and table – that revolves at the press of a button.

31

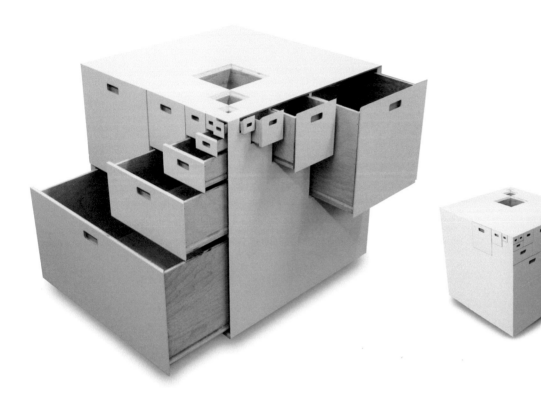

TAKESHI MIYAKAWA
Fractal 23 storage
A playful modular drawer system that can be opened from all four sides. The various sizes and shapes of each compartment demand that a user consider more carefully what should be stored there.

CENTRALA
Softbox environment
Every patch in this patchwork cube opens to reveal storage and hidden household appliances.

NAOKI HIRAKOSO

1 H 03 storage
The designer gave the traditional chest of drawers a contemporary arching form, that gives the object a feeling of stability, while retaining the light feel of paulownia wood.

2 Kai table
The name of this table – made in collaboration with Takamitsu Kitahara – is a Sino-Japanese word that signifies a personal space since the measurement and configuration of its compartments can be customised.

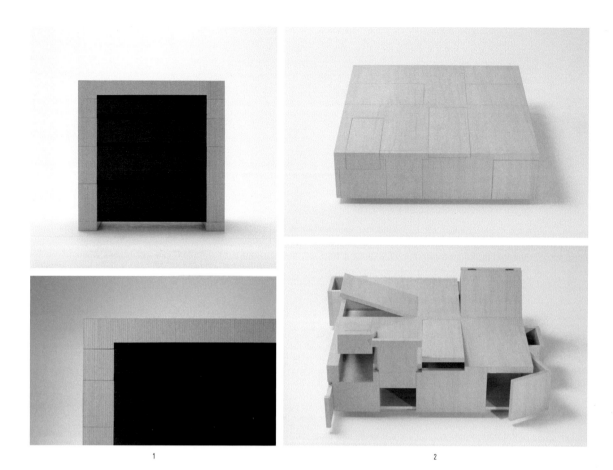

1

2

NAOKI HIRAKOSO

H 01 storage
This TV cabinet was made for Paulownia, a brand that specialises in chests made of the exquisitely straight-grained paulownia wood and a collaboration between the Kamo Chest Manufacturer's Cooperative and a group of emerging Japanese designers called GIBA. A concealed hinge allows the cabinet doors to open in unusual directions.

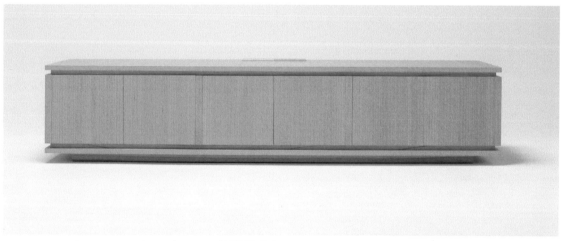

1

2

1 Cork chair
Produced in a limited edition of 25,
Morrison's supremely simplified seat is
made from wine bottle corks.

NEO DESIGN
Rodrigo Vairinhos
2 Corky Lips chair
This designer uses sensual, pleasing
shapes to promote the use of organic
and recyclable materials. Corky Lips
are made from recyclable foam upholstered with cork leather. The manufacturing process produces almost no
waste or toxic emissions.

NAOKI HIRAKOSO
Trapez table

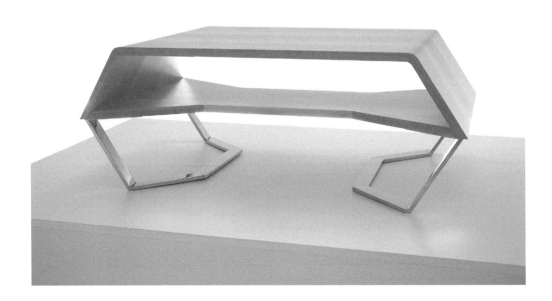

NAOKI HIRAKOSO
1 LINUM Series
2 LINUM 100
3 LINUM Aluminium 50
The lines of this nesting low table and stool group are more elegant for being so slender. At first glance, the material looks like plywood, but the structure is actually supported by 4 mm-thick aluminium plates.

VIABLE LONDON
4 Selflife desk
A compliment to an earlier Shelflife unit, the Shelflife desk replaces the chair and side table of the original with a workspace and seating. The piece is designed for the home-office, which usually lacks the square footage needed for a dedicated desk.

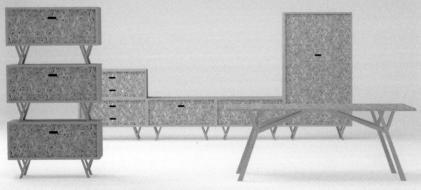

1

2

4

3

6

5

BIHAIN
Michaël Bihain

1 Libri shelving
A storage solution suited to the modern-day nomadic lifestyle, Libri can be used as a single unit attached to the wall or combined with additional shelves on the wall or in the middle of the room to create a partition. Its legs can be adjusted individually (even after being attached to the wall or to each other) to conform to uneven floors.

DUSTDELUXE
Damien Gernay & Jeremy Vanneste

2 Playtime shelf
Playtime is a modular shelf referring to the structured and colourful universe of Jacques Tati's eponymous film in which an aseptic environment and architecture imbue life with cold rationality against which warmer human instincts struggle. Playtime modules can be adjusted in height and position and composed in multiple ways.

MIN CHEN
3 Stereo Calligraphy – "Gong" table
"Gong" means labour, work, project, and skill in Chinese. Its shape comes from ancient architectural structures and joinery tools.

1

2

3

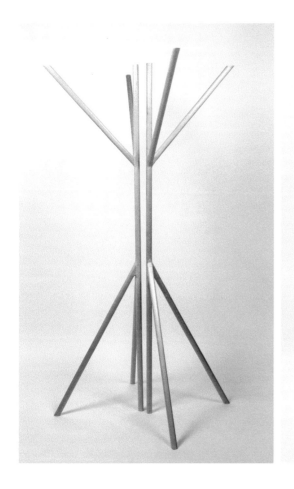

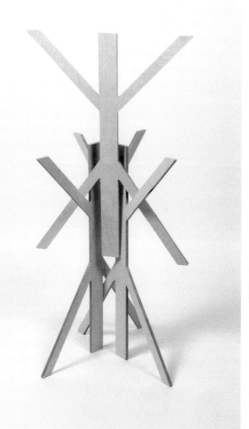

1

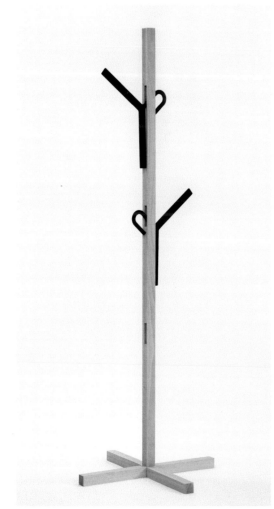

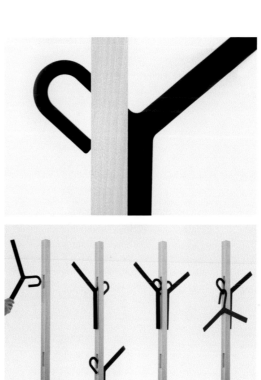

MIN CHEN
1 Stereo Calligraphy – "Mu" rack
"Mu" means wood in Chinese. It represents the shape of a tree's bole with
branches on the top and a root at the
bottom. Two "Mu" compose the character "Lin", which means forest. Three
"Mu" make up the character "Sen",
which means full of trees.

TAKASHI SATO
2 Coat Hanger
This coat hanger uses a hanger as its
structure, offering a variety of ways to
use the piece.

2

1

2

PATRICK NORGUET
1 Silvera Collection 01
2 Nao stools
3 Folio desk
4 Spirit stool

3

4

MICHAEL YOUNG
1   Capra stool

PHILIP EDIS
2   Twist table/storage
    Twist is both a table and a shelf, inspired
    by the hula-hoop: in the same way that the
    hoop rotates around the body, the boards
    rotate around an axis.

PATRICK NORGUET
3   Element centrepiece

1

2

3

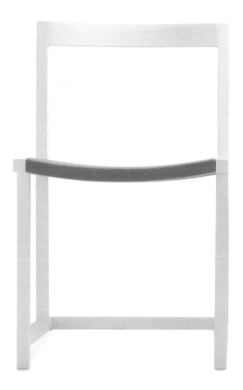

FOR USE

1 90° chair
The profile of the chair consists of four mutually orthogonal bars, each of them longer than the adjoining bar. The armchair is achieved through the addition of two additional orthogonal bars, one of them an extension of the front leg.

NEO DESIGN
Rodrigo Vairinhos

2 V.chair
The design of this beechwood, lacquer-finished chair is a direct response to the demands of the production line.

JASPER MORRISON

3 Basel chair
Designed for Vitra, this wooden chair features a seat and back in dyed-through plastic.

1

2

3

BARBER OSGERBY

1   Delta table

For Established & Sons, Delta grew out of the observation that a triangular shape fits into many interior scenarios. It can stand alone, next to a wall or beside another piece of furniture. The low table can serve as a coffee table, bedside table or stool. The higher version can be paired with an easy chair or sofa, as an occasional table or a plinth. The tables are cast from a hollow-core resin that provides a high gloss finish and unusual depth.

PATRICK NORGUET

2,4 Lila stool

MIKIYA KOBAYASHI

3   Ceppo stool

A stool with a ring-shaped seat that can be easily carried by grabbing the seat.

1

2

3

4

43

BARBER OSGERBY

1 De La Warr Pavilion chair
Originally created to furnish the De La
Warr Pavilion, one of England's most
famous Modernist buildings, the rectilinear volumes of which demanded a
sculptural solution, this chair is made
from high-pressure, die-cast aluminum. A radiused rear skid leg contrasts
with the hard lines of the building's
interior. Its front legs and arms are made
from steel or stainless steel tubing
while the seat and back use a special
ductile grade aluminum, which are
pressed into shape either with or without holes. The holes reduce the weight
of the chair, help to increase its structural integrity and reduce wind drag for
the outdoor version. It is also available
upholstered in fabric or leather.

NAOKI HIRAKOSO

2 Linum Rod table
Slimmed down veneer hides the 4 mm-
thick steel support that allows the furniture to look so slender and soft.

AUTOBAN
Seyhan Özdemir, Sefer Çağlar
3 Pebble table
With legs made from plate iron and
an organic-shaped wooden top, Pebble
unites opposites.

1

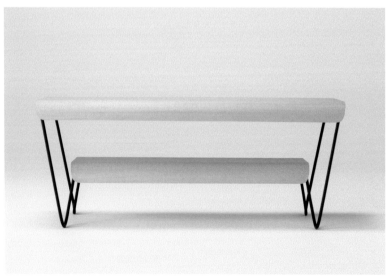

2

3

FOR USE
1   Satyr chair
    Two similar triangular profiles form the
    seat and the backrest and are rotated
    at 90°, gathering the greatest thickness
    at the back of the seat and top of the
    backrest, the areas of highest pressure
    during use. The flat profiles of the base
    are split in half, providing support for
    both seat and backrest.

FORMFJORD
2   Daybed B194
    A surprising interpretation of uphol-
    stered furniture, this slatted bench-like
    daybed combines a simple appearance
    with a high level of comfort.

STUDIOILSE
    Ilse Crawford
3   Studiolise w08
    Crawford's sturdy, unpretentious light
    is made from an odd combination of
    materials that she makes work: iron to
    convey stability and reliability, wood
    for its warmth and porcelain for its in-
    timacy, tactility and glow. The quirki-
    ness of the material palette, according
    to the designer, heightens the innate
    awkwardness of the directional light.

1

2

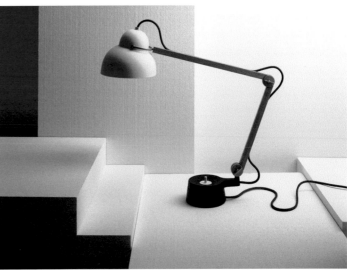

3

HANNES WETTSTEIN
Pages 25, 46, 62

Zürich-based designer Hannes Wettstein used to win Red Dot and iF awards so regularly that organisers probably should have considered excluding him from the running in fairness to the competition. Establishing his own studio in 1982, Wettstein's work featured clean lines, satisfying curves and folds and a curious alternation between dematerialisation and bulk, darkness and light.

Baleri manufactured his skinny Juliette folding chair in 1987. Wettstein's sliver-thin, facet-legged Alfa chairs and tables were made for Molteni in 2001. Their allusion to the two-dimensional returned four years later with the round-topped Tika table, produced by Interna. Featuring black surfaces lined with white edges, Tika looks as if it has been unfolded from cut paper, a 2D object that nonetheless has surprising mass. The Vela for Accademia looks feather-light, on the other hand: a slim tubular aluminum frame extends slightly to form small wings and is wrapped with a large-knit textile. The stacking Tototo chair for MaxDesign, with its soft double-walled bucket seat and leggy profile, won the 2007 Good Design Award.

But the designer also dabbled in product design (from medical equipment and massage chairs to telescopes and watches) and the interior design of TV sets, hotels, offices and residential space, including the polished interiors of architect Steven Holl's Swiss Embassy in Washington, D.C.

In 2007, Wettstein, who died the following year, launched the interdisciplinary laboratory zed in order to promote ideas and work that he did not want bound to his own name. The source, however, was fairly obvious.

Tototo chair
This beautiful bucket for Maxdesign is all frame. Injection moulded in polypropylene, it comes in a rainbow of colours and can be stacked to the sky.

1

2

3

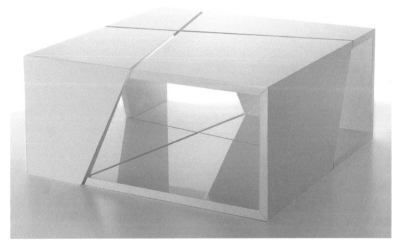

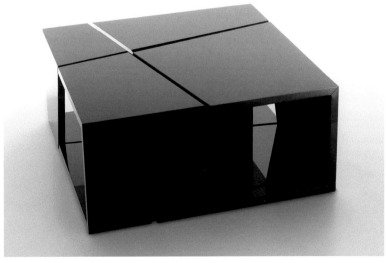

4

CHRISTOPHE DELCOURT OBJETS /MOBILIER
Christophe Delcourt
1 ALP lamp

TAKASHI SATO
2 Tongs table lamp
The structure of this table lamp sandwiches the electric bulb socket in a way inspired by the highly useful kitchen tool.

ADRIEN ROVERO
3 Pimp stool and low table
This stool and table are based on an simple construction principle: a standard H profile and a folded sheet that becomes the connecting element. The anodisation of the aluminum, a process typically used in the "tunning" car industry, lends a particular shiny quality that adds to the product's simplicity.

VOONWONG&BENSONSAW
4 Slicebox coffee table
A square coffee tabletop is incised with random cuts and actually sliced through to form smaller units that serve as side tables of different shapes and dimensions.

1

2

3

4

5

MIKKO LAAKKONEN

1 Latva coatrack
2 Latva Wall coatrack
Stand-alone and wall-mounted coat-racks pay homage to traditional Nordic wood decoration techniques.

ADRIEN ROVERO

3 Cabane Perchée shelter
This installation was made for the parklands surrounding the castle of Ferté Vidame located south of Paris. In 2006, three designers (5.5designers, Normal Studio and Adrien Rovero) were commissioned to create quiet spots for visitors to rest on the grounds. Rovero's piece resembles a huge bird-house (visitors can sit inside) which lent whimsy and played with the scale of the surroundings since three normal birdhouses are also on display nearby to emphasise the contradiction.

FREDRIK MATTSON

4 TBC – The Black Chair Collection
A hardwood chair collection made in an environmentally friendly way, using the hardwood that normally is rejected due to colour shades or other beauty defects.

5 Babel table and TBC 1 chair
7 Babel table
A table which can play an important role in an interior, instead of just being the servant to the chosen chair.

PETER BRANDT

6 Bimbo stool
A stool that is easy to bring with you and that can be stored on a limited surface and placed anywhere.

1

2

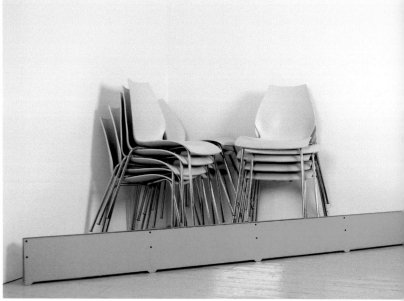

3

ADRIEN ROVERO
1   Portique reading light
This object defines a quiet reading space while providing good light and allowing the reader to pull their favourite seat underneath.

PATRICK GAVIN
2,3   Room Divider
Taking its inspiration from wet floor signs and supermarket checkout grocery dividers, "Room Divider" implies a simple boundary in an interior. The black walnut wooden spine identifies it as a piece of furniture, while the bright green powder-coated aluminum sides and exposed fasteners suggest a more industrious application. Combining the considered with the banal and the designed with the engineered aesthetic, "Room Divider" and its unusual proportions propose new ways of organising possessions in domestic or public space.

PATRICK GAVIN

1,2 Basic Boundaries
Basic Boundaries divides a room, either
enclosing a smaller space or splitting
a larger space in two, and using colour
and pattern to further define separate
zones. Reacting to the banality of most
architectural environments, it questions how people interact with objects
and subsequently with each other.

TAF
Gabriella Gustafson & Mattias Ståhlbom
3   Room Divider
4   Trestle table legs/room partition

1

2

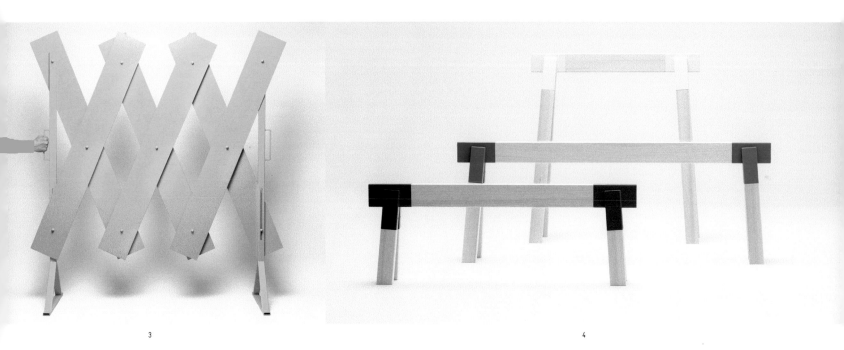

3

4

1

STUDIO GORM
John Arndt

1 Camp installation
An installation with various furniture elements, camp desk, plug/lamp post laptop bag and k-bright light.

2 Lighting/Bug
"A lamp with no fixed agenda, it doesn't like to stay in one place, but would rather confound the flies trying to fly around it." The light created by these single-engine-plane LED lights flits a-round to create shifting shadows. The speed of the blades can also be adjusted to one's preference.

3 Camp/Bench
This seating references the lightweight structure typical of camping equipment but adds the comfort and style that are usually stripped away for the sake of functionality. Even if the piece is only momentarily in use and can be folded up quickly (and even hung on a wall where it creates a lovely graphic), it has been made as comfortable and inviting as possible.

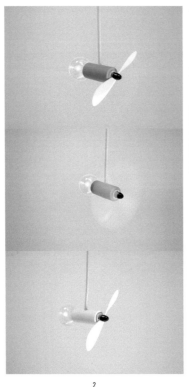

2

3

1

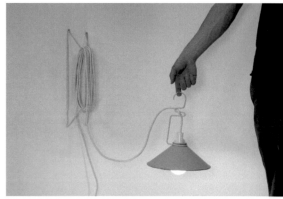

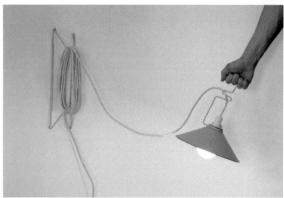

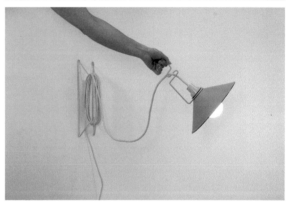

3

2

STUDIO GORM
John Arndt

1   Pole/Plug/Lamp
A variation on the Plug/Lamp (below),
Pole/Plug is adjustable for height and
direction. Its long, bright cord allows
the light to be placed in the middle of
rooms where outlets may not be within
easy reach.

2,3 Plug/Lamp
This lamp celebrates the humble, banal
and undersung beauty of the extension
cord. By clamping a simple shade to the
cord and fixing a light socket to a plug,
Arndt allows users to convert any extension cord into a handsome, utilitarian lamp. A rack keeps the cord coiled
tidily while a hook allows the shade to
be hung wherever needed.

JÖRG BONER
Page 54

Swiss product designer Jörg Boner's Universal resembles a stool, a low-slung table and a fold-up drying rack simultaneously. Its design (for temporary-addorisio in 2007) was an exercise in seeing just how far Boner could distance form from function. In fact, Boner never does explain the use of Universal. Made from 1.5 mm sheet metal in limited edition, it might serve several purposes, domestic or commercial, but Boner leaves it to the end-user to decide. It seems safe to say that Boner's design is dictated less by the immediate desire to solve a problem than by the desire to create an even more interesting problem.

Boner earned his 1996 diploma from the former Schule für Gestaltung (School for Design) in Basel. Follow graduation, he cofounded the N2 collective with Valerie Kiock, Kuno Nüssli, Christian Deuber, Paolo Fasulo, This Reber and Dave Braun. But by 2001 he had established Jörg Boner productdesign in Zürich and, a year later, joined the faculty at the Ecole Cantonale d'Art de Lausanne (ECAL).

In 2007, instead of upholstering his Wogg 42 chair, he dressed it: the drape of a narrow folded strip of fabric – anchored in place with a system of press-studs, this textile can be easily exchanged for another – forming both seat and backrest. In 2008, Boner has also slotted together a satisfyingly puzzle-like prototype lamp called Champignon which is made, as unlikely as it may sound, from cardboard. One hopes it will be sold in a flat-pack kit.

1 Wogg 42 chair
   Boner placed upholstery over the chair's frame like a dress. The textiles were made in an industrial process that involved high-frequency welding. Fixed with press-studs, they are easily interchangeable, in turn changing the chair's expression according to the colour and material used.

2 Universal object
   Made of 1.5 mm folded and welded sheet steel in two sizes, these objects are reminiscent of industrial objects, tables, side tables, racks or stools. Boner leaves their function to be determined by the user.

3 Champagnon table lamp
   A prototype cardboard light produces an intimate warm glow and somehow mimics the look of a Tiffany lamp.

3

BARBER OSGERBY

Pages 43–44, 55, 235

BarberOsgerby are brilliant formalists. This can be seen in the most simple of pieces they produce, such as the Tab lamp for Flos, a rudimentary folded shape that works on desk, wall or floor. Also basic but striking in form was the pair's 2007 Bottle table in marble, made for Cappellini but revisited a year later in handblown glass (requiring one of the largest glass moulds in existence) for the extremely high-end Meta by Mallett line. Their Delta table, manufactured in resin for Established & Sons began with the observation that a triangular objects can be easily integrated into any interior.

Not surprising then that it was architecture that Edward Barber and Jay Osgerby studied at London's Royal College of Art. They set up shop together in 1996, Giulio Cappellini discovered them in 1998, and they began to churn out everything from cathedral interiors and Levis clothes hangers to beverage bottles and shop interiors. The studio was commissioned to design furniture for the De La Warr Pavilion, one of the UK's most beloved Modernist buildings. The industrial and yet sculptural-looking chairs they made featured hard lines coupled with a radiused skid leg and soft perforations of the backrest. The De La Warr chairs were produced for the building in a brilliant powder-coated red/orange but also made in white, black and a vivid clover green by Established & Sons.

The designers' strengths don't stop at form: they have proven themselves brilliant colourists as well. The 2008 IRIS series for Established & Sons features five low tables, each in a different colour spectrum. The word "iris" refers to the coloured portion of the eye and to a rainbow but the collection is really a celebration of the colour chart. Sometimes the many colours ranging the sides of each table are a graduated run of similar tones; others are arranged to emphasise tonal differences. The juxtaposition of colours was meticulously chosen to ensure that adjacent colours compliment one another. The effect is as close as one can get to having a rainbow without rain.

1 Saturn stool
This lacquered solid-wood stool supplements its predecessor, a coat stand (below), using elliptical rings as its base.

2 Saturn coat stand
A solid-timber coat stand comprising six interlocking geometric arcs designed for Classicon.

3 Zero-In coffee table
This Pop Art-looking table is made from a polyester-moulding compound compressed in a metal mould, a process standard to the car industry in the manufacture of body panels, which, when painted, are indistinguishable from metal components.

4 Birds on a Wire coat rack
A coat rack taking its cues from Shaker peg rails, this piece attaches to a wall-mounted rail. Interconnectors allow users to run the rail around an entire room, if desired.

5 Tab lamp
This lamp is a simple folded form that has desk, wall and floor versions, all with rotatable shade. The simplicity of the form contrasts with the high-tech ceramic reflector that gives glareless illumination.

1

2

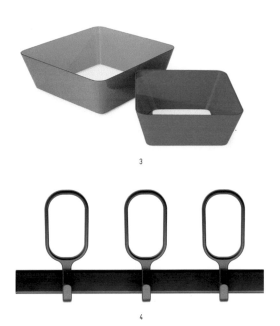

3

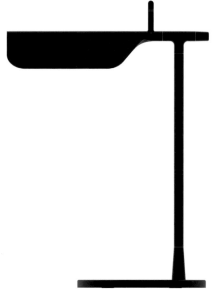

4

5

GUILLAUME DELVIGNE
Page 56

Like a DNA scientist, Guillaume Delvigne preserves bits and pieces of classic forms but mischievously draws these genes and textures out of their typical context and assigns them to a wholly unexpected one. Working with fellow French designer Ionna Vautrin, Delvigne produced the now recognisable Panier Percé series – simple white ceramic bowls densely perforated, like a needlepoint pattern, to hold wool thread – with ratatouille, jacquard, pixelated and other patterns. Appropriating an entirely unlikely material (yarn used in modern tabletop design?) and combining it with an entirely unlikely mate (yarn threaded through porcelain?) is typical of Delvigne's fascinating investigations and patchwork production. What makes the experiments so successful is the seamlessness and sophistication that marks the finished product.

Delvigne (1979) studied industrial design in Nantes and Milan. On graduating in 2002, he began to collaborate with George J. Sowden, later moving to Paris to work with RADI Designers, Delo Lindo and Robert Stadler. In 2004 Delvigne participated in the first Industreal exhibition, In Dust We Trust, and since then has designed several pieces produced by the Milanese collective. Delvigne is currently on staff in the Mark Newson studio is a founding member of the design collective Dito.

In 2007, for Italian collective Industreal, Delvigne produced the Les Vases Texturés series: the cookie jar-shaped and waffle-skinned Vase Gaufré and the Vase Capitonné with the tufts and puckers of a Chesterfield sofa. This year, he created the basket-like Rombas vases with thick porcelain handles and blown – vividly coloured – glass "baskets." He used the same materials for the periscopic Fabbrica del Vapore vases and the twin bells of the Donges centrepiece. Delvigne continues to prove himself an unerring hand at choosing colours, forms, compositions, materials, in short, at selecting the genetic markers that will have the greatest success and tossing the rest.

GUILLAUME DELVIGNE & IONNA VAUTRIN
1 Donges 01 centrepiece
2 Donges 02 centrepiece
3 Fabbrica Del Vapore vases
4 Donges 03 centrepiece
5 Rombas vases

1

2

3

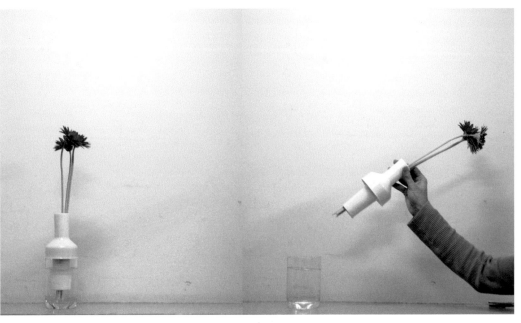

4

MARK BRAUN

1 Fusion
Fusion is a response to the change of our use and the intention of tableware, serving all kinds of dishes on the same dishes. It comes in six colours by ASA Selection and contrasts matt and velvety glazes on the exterior with a shiny porcelain interior.

2 Ova glass/egg cup
Ova glass series hones your decision making skills, converting from glass to egg cup. The series plays with this double function in an effort to demonstrate that a shape can be beautiful even if turned the "wrong" way around.

FRONT

3 Glass table
Inspired by a passage from Lewis Carroll's Alice in Wonderland when Alice discovers a little table made of solid glass with a tiny golden key and a little bottle with the words "DRINK ME": "'What a curious feeling!' said Alice... She was now only ten inches high... When she got to the door, she found she had forgotten the little golden key, and when she went back to the table for it, she found she could not possibly reach it: she could see it quite plainly through the glass."

TAKASHI SATO

4 Kaki vase
This vase comes apart at its center, allowing the water to be changed without disturbing the flower arrangement.

PATRICK NORGUET

Pages 24, 26, 40–41, 43, 58–59

Patrick Norguet is a manufacturer's designer: pragmatic, prolific, clever, an engineer before an aesthete and a maker without conceptual hangups. The Paris-based freelance product designer tends to churn out furniture for the likes of Moroso, Bernhardt, Poltrona Frau, Thonet and Frighetto that can safely be assumed to become modern classics in a few years' time.

Since 1998, Norguet has been creating everything from window displays and scenography for legends like Louis Vuitton, Givenchy and Guerlain (and relative youngsters like Girbaud and Martine Sitbon) to products such as candles, lamps and scent diffusers. And then there are the Lancel boutiques and Renault showrooms.

It was in 2000 that Giulio Cappellini gave Norguet his big break in furniture, producing his striped plastic Rainbow chair and, a year later, his Rive Droite seating system which used Emilio Pucci fabric upholstery. But these two projects were much more decorative than is standard for Norguet.

More typical of the designer, perhaps, are minimal pieces featuring clever details. His Apollo armchair, an immediately recognisable homage to French design master Pierre Paulin, brought Artifort success in 2002. In 2008, he produced the quilted Bend armchair and swivel seat for Fasem. A set of low metal end tables, called Fold for Modus, have a pared-down austerity.

But Norguet's four-piece Edition 01 collection for Paris' Silvera best encapsulates the designer's signature anti-flourishes: the reduction of forms, the lack of needless extras, the combination of materials that render classics entirely modern, the subtle but brilliant details. The star of the collection is surely the Folio desk with its curved plane of neoprene colliding with a slender, sharp plane of oak. It becomes quickly clear: Norguet is in the details.

1

2

DIRK WINKEL

1 Discu table
   A lightweight, straightforward table
   series with a flat sheet steel base.
   The base's geometrical symmetry and
   construction are a new take on the
   principles of L-profile steel construction, ensuring ultra-high stability and
   low weight.

2 Minai sofa

3 Minai easy chair
   This miniature two-seater and easy
   chair are as comfortable as their larger
   counterparts. Their central aluminum
   bars allow different kind of shells
   (wood or upholstered aluminum) to be
   clamped in.

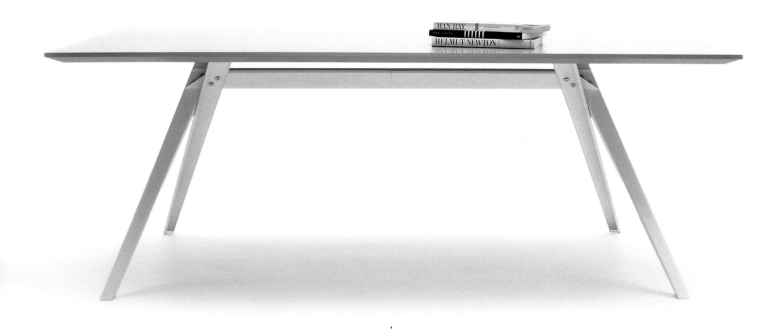

1

2

3

STEFAN BORSELIUS
Peekaboo chair
The smallest of rooms. In times when we
break down existing barriers to facilitate
meetings and shared encounters, new needs
for seclusion soon arise.

HANNES WETTSTEIN

1 Vela chair
Vela comes as an armchair and chaise longue. The stackable steel-tube frame can be galvanised and lacquered in various colours and is suitable for indoor or outdoor use. The seat and back are gracefully woven in rope for interiors, or in PVC rope for either in or out.

DUSTDELUXE
Damien Gernay

2 STRUKTr table
3 STRUKTr chair
The two lacquered aluminum sheets that make up the STRUKTr chair and table sandwich injected epoxy foam. The physical properties of the foam, its alveolar structure, its adherence and its low expansion pressure lend the table strength while keeping its weight down.

4 Barnum desk

1

2

3

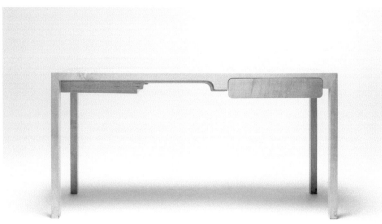

4

FOR USE

1 Riva chair
While the 500 m waterfront in Split/Croatia was being reconstructed and refurnished in collaboration with the architects 3LHD in 2007, For Use developed an outdoor chair for the project. The continuous frame of the legs and armrests is made of 14 mm tubular steel, while the parallel seat and backrest bars are made of 7 mm steel rod.

JUNIO DESIGN
Jun Hashimoto

2 Thin table
3,4 Thin chair
A chair and table in their most reduced forms, created by bending single sheets of steel.

1

2

3

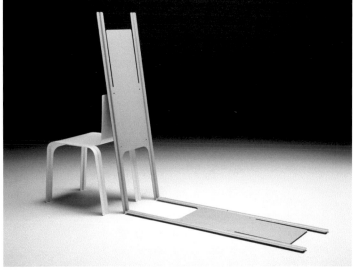

4

SAMARE
M. Bedikian, L. Bedikian,
N. Bellavance-LeCompte,
P. Meirim de Barros

The young Montreal-based design collective, Samare, takes its name from the winged fruit of the maple tree that disperses its seeds on the wind. Samare's four-person team consists of two architects and two designers (one of whom is based in Milan) and focuses on Canadian cultural symbols to translate them into contemporary design. Laurie Bedikian (who studied at Central St. Martins), Mania Bedikian, Patrick Meirim de Barros and Nicolas Bellavance-LeCompte launched their first collection, Awadare: We Live In, in 2008, using Aboriginal methods for treating and weaving babiche, a natural leather hind typically used in snowshoe laces worn by Canadian fur trappers for centuries.

Samare's preservation of their cultural heritage lends the collection authenticity, and a grace that the vernacular weaving gives to the cane-like surfaces. In the chairs, in particular, they have preserved the classic proportions but pared them down to a slim minimum, including the high-backed Capitaine, the throne-like Métis and the low-slung laid-back chaise longue called Mush! to which they have added an unusual triangular switchback detail in the front legs. The Mountie ("we stand guard for thee") stool, appropriately, is rendered in bright red metal. The tables seem to draw on mid-century Modernist forms: Federal is a bilevel coffee table while the Glide side table cantilevers proudly over a single leg. The world (and the design industry) could do with more of Samare's brand of nationalism.

1

1 Federal secretary/
  console and Métis chair
  Samare says it best: This piece will
  unify all of your "life's major acts and
  treaties," and become the element
  governing any room.

2 Provincial table and
  Territory stackable chairs

3 Chaise Capitaine
  An interpretation of a historically
  designed low-back wooden armchair,
  originally imported from England, but
  popularised in French-speaking Canada
  after it became part of the Common-
  wealth. The change in proportions makes
  it ideal for sitting at the head of the
  table or for a throne-like experience.

4 Mush! lounge chair and
  Glide side table
  With a base like a ski runner, a back
  support like a drive bow, a leg support
  like a brush bow and a seat made from
  a continuous babiche basket weave,
  Mush! is a lounge chair based on a dog
  sleigh. Its side table is called Glide.

5 Federal secretary/console
  Entire collection woven from babiche
  hide, a native technique.

3

2

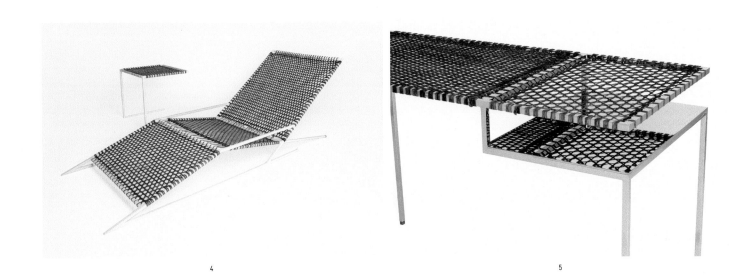

4

5

1

2

KURSI
Abdul Ghafoor

1 Sideboard
This sideboard is a throwback to 1950s
furniture, reminiscent of the works
of mid-century designers such as Paul
McCobb. The modern twist, however,
is a projecting volume inspired by
the architectural edifice of the Royal
Library in Copenhagen. Sideboard's
surfaces are also divided according to
the Golden Ratio.

FURNITURE FOR DAILY USE
Martin Holzapfel

2 Bureau desk
This piece combines a desk with a shelf
that rests on the work surface.

LIFEGOODS

3 2-20 desk
A desk for anyone between 2 and 20
years of age.

4 Shelves "Serie"
A shelving system made of 20mm plywood that consists of two trestles and
a box. Depending on the way it is positioned, the box can either be used as
shelving or as storage. When tilted, it
can serve as a rack in which to display
and store magazines.

5 Table "Serie"
This trestle table is made of 300mm
plywood, the compact trestles and top
of which can be converted into a con-
ference table, desk, or dining table.

6 "Serie"
Serie is an ongoing project that began
in 2006 and is based on furthering
the notions of mobility and versatility
through furniture design.

3

4
5

6

ECAL/RAPHAËL VON ALLMEN

1 Plastic-Back Chair
A chair in plastic and aluminium made using techniques such as welding, laser cutting and CNC milling. This means that the chair doesn't require expensive equipment and can be produced in small quantities.

RONAN & ERWAN BOUROULLEC

2,3 Steelwood Collection
The Steelwood pieces are assemblages of two traditional materials (metal and plastic) that are intended to become more pliable over time. The difficult curvature of the metal piece was produced in a 10-step stamping process.

1

2

3

1

2

4

3

LIFEGOODS
1 Table Basse
This steel table can be folded and clamped by the user.

TAKASHI SATO
2 Pata stool
A folding stool that morphs between three dimensional and two dimensional shapes.

GEOFFREY LILGE
3 L 40 lounge chair
4 L 41 armchair
With solid maple frames and Bendy-wood components, these two lounge chair prototypes feature bent plywood and fiberglass seats and backs.

1

MARK BRAUN

1 Lingor lights
The suspension light series Lingor is manufactured using a traditional metal compression process – and phosphorescent enamel. The pieces have modern shaping, sustainable characteristics and are suited to various lighting needs from spotlighting to diffusing light.

NEO DESIGN
Rodrigo Vairinhos

2 Small Light Collection
A group of four geometrically refined hanging spot lamps made in ceramic. Available in black and/or white with high gloss surfaces.

2

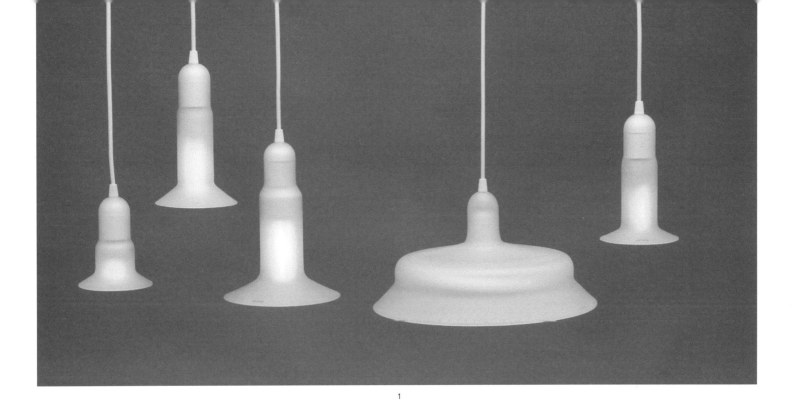

1

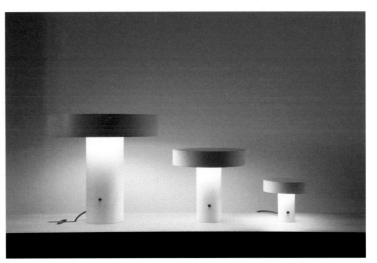

2

ADRIEN ROVERO
1 Saving Grace lamps
Rovero's series of sheer lampshades
were adapted to the diverse and quirky
shapes of energy-saving bulbs.

LIFEGOODS
2 3x lamps
Though they don't look it, these lamps
were made from existing steel pipes.

RONAN & ERWAN BOUROULLEC
Galerie Kreo solo exhibition, 2008

1

RONAN & ERWAN BOUROULLEC
1 Galerie Kreo exhibition, Blacklight
2 Galerie Kreo exhibition, Sofa

2

FABIEN CAPPELLO
Page 75

Based between Paris and London while studying at the Royal College of Art, product and exhibition designer Fabien Cappello produced a series of lights in 2007 that were spartan in form and surehandedly elegant in their composition. With its slender L shape, his ceiling-mounted, chromed metal wire pendant light (the bulb being all the pendant there is) is as irreducible as a prime number. Nonetheless, it is Cappello's limited-edition Sandcast lamp, presented at Villa Noailles in Hyeres during Design Parade 2007, that may generate the most buzz.

Cappello's process was based on an aluminium sand-casting technique that produces unique objects through a serial process. He created a model of the table light in expanded polystyrene that he recycled from fragments of packaging that had once contained household appliances but were thrown away by local supermarkets. He then cut up the salvaged foam, reassembled the pieces and moulded this patchwork form to create a functional lamp. "My purpose was to take advantage of existing objects by stealing their formal character for unique use," the designer explains. "Released from any classic editorial constraint, the objects are irregular, their details raw and unfinished."

1. Sandcast lamp
   Cappello used an aluminum sandcasting technique to make unique lights through a serial process. He created a model of the table light in expanded poly-styrene salvaged from packaging, cut up and reassembled into the lamp's form before being moulded.

2. Ceiling-mounted light
3. Wireclip lighting system

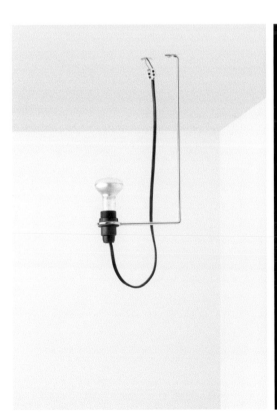

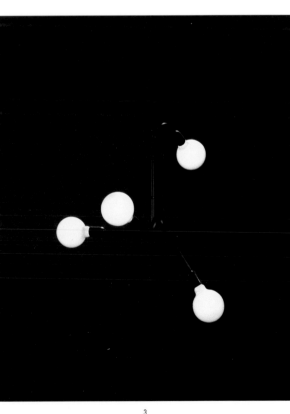

ALAIN GILLES

1 Rock Garden planter
Gilles' planters resemble pieces of a
path made from roughly-cut stones.
The user can play with these modular
units to design their own garden indoors or outdoors.

2 Connnectivity Island bench/planter
For Urbastyle, Gilles created a concrete
bench and planters based on combina-
tory logic. The repetition and juxtaposition of identical elements sometimes
generates the unexpected. The two pieces can be produced in the same moulds
because they share most of their parts.

RONAN & ERWAN BOUROULLEC

3 Galerie Kreo exhibition, Banquise bench

1

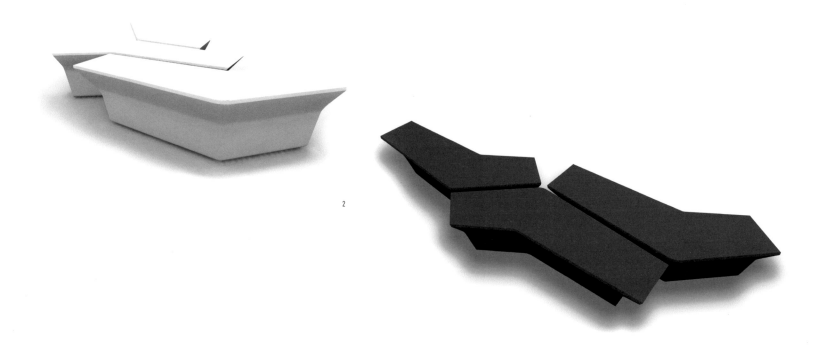

2

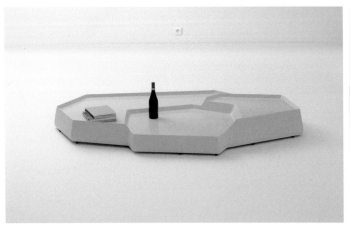
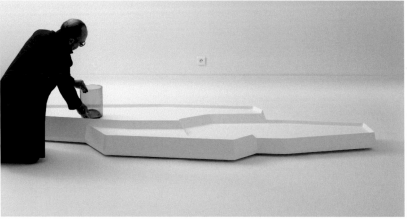

3

FORM US WITH LOVE
Prosthesis coatrack
Why buy more when we've got so much already? The designers urge consumers to buy the connection joint and add their own prostheses – a hockey stick, a broom, a spare branch – to create a coatrack from existing objects.

PATRICIA URQUIOLA
1   Re-Trouvée outdoor seating

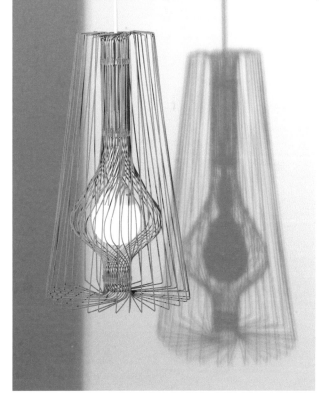

3

4

EVA MARGUERRE
Nido stool and table

Marguerre fixed the coordinates describing the shape of a stool in space and connected them with fibreglass and later soaked with dyed polyester resin. The method generates unique patterns and structures and therefore unique stools or tables. The resulting pieces are also both extremely light and stable.

ALAIN GILLES

1 Tectonic side table and sofa
The Tectonic series for Bonaldo is based on the idea of movement during the construction of its shape. Gilles' tables combine plastic and graphic approaches to the design. The pieces are made from metal wire, or with a plain top that has been laser-cut from a 4mm steel sheet and then powder-coated in a matt finish.

VOONWONG&BENSONSAW

2 Tripod stool
Constructed from three U-shaped supports of 8mm steel rod, the Tripod stools are reinforced with three identical diagonal braces that also act as footrests. Tripod is available in either bar or kitchen height, with a padded or mesh seat.

ALEXANDER LERVIK

3 The Red Chair
Made from seven lacquered steel sticks, the red chair was originally shown in the "Five Playful Chairs" exhibition in 2005 in a limited edition of 10.

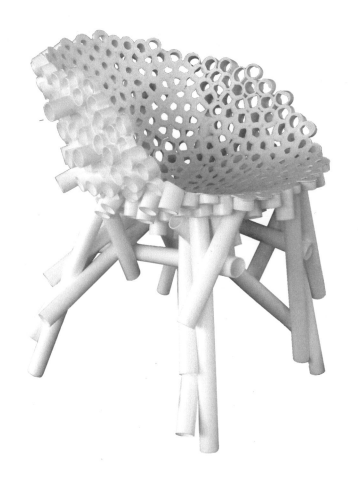

THE INVENTORS

SLIM LINE / ART NOUVEAU / STEALTH / VIRUS ATTACKS / FRAMEWORK / INTERACTION / ORGANIC FORM / DIGITAL LIFE

ADRIEN ROVERO / ALEXANDER KNELLER / AMANDA LEVETE / ANTHONY DICKENS / BAS VAN DER VEER / BRAM BOO / CARL OJERSTAM / CORDULA KEHRER / CRIS BARTELS / DAVE KEUNE / DEF-DEF. / DAVID TRUBRIDGE / DICKENS&WILSON / FOR USE / GARETH NEAL / JASON MILLER / JULIA LOHMANN / JULIAN MAYOR / KONSTANTIN GRCIC INDUSTRIAL DESIGN / MAARTEN BAAS / MARK BRAUN / MATTHIAS BÄR / MATHIAS BENGTSSON / MATHIEU LEHANNEUR / MICHAEL BIHAIN / MATTHIAS-STUDIO / MAX LAMB / NACHO CARBONELL / NENDO / O-D-A / OSKAR ZIETA / PATRICIA URQUIOLA / PAUL LOEBACH / PHILIP MICHAEL WOLFSON / PIEKE BERGMANS / PLATFORM STU-DIO / R&SIE / RAPHAËL VON ALLMEN / STEPHEN BURKS / RICCARDO BLUMER / MATTEO BORGHI / SHAY ALKALAY / STEFAN DIEZ / STEVEN HOLL ARCHITECTS / STUDIO LIBERTINY / TAKESHI MIYAKAWA / THOMAS FEICHTNER / TOMITA KAZUHIKO / TOM PRICE / YAEL MER

INVENTORS WANT TO REVOLUTIONISE CONSTRUCTION, QUESTION TECHNIQUES, TRY OUT MATERIALS. THEY BELIEVE THAT THINGS CAN GET BETTER. THEY ARE INTERESTED ONLY PERIPHERALLY IN AESTHETICS.

Admittedly: there are times when interested watchers of design events are beset by a creeping but vivid fear that the discipline is going the best way about abolishing itself. It seems that the stranglehold of marketing is so strong that it is reducing design to a compliant instrument that can create added value for even the most superfluous of products. But there is always hope: alongside all those who are most concerned with taking themselves seriously, there are still designers who take their profession seriously in the first place. This is a seriousness that could be experienced in KONSTANTIN GRCIC'S chair for Plank, for example. What made it into something exceptional at the 2008 Milan Furniture Fair? There are thousands of cantilever chairs, good ones and bad ones, but the last person to look at the idea of a plastic cantilever chair – a material that was somewhat brittle at the time – was Verner Panton, 40 years ago. He created the prototype of the Monoblock cantilever chair, a design that scarcely anyone has dared to touch since then.

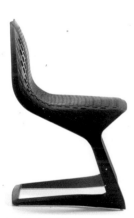

Konstantin Grcic / Myto

On the other hand, we now have different plastics with properties that permit different designs and innovative construction principles. It is possible to create shaped products appropriate to our times that can enrich our everyday culture freshly and vigorously. This is precisely the approach that inventors take. They are the prototypes of designers who seem to torment themselves with almost antiquated questions about meaning. They are concerned to develop the best possible form for a product from the point of view of the creative individual – to find an up-to-date material, an up-to-date form or an up-to-date process on the basis of an individual consumer need, so that this need can be met in the best possible way. Inventors rack their brains tirelessly, they are explorers, entrepreneurs, people who are trying to make things as good as they can possibly be, people who are not blinkered against either industry or craft. They want to revolutionise construction, question techniques, try out materials. They believe that things can get better. They

are interested only peripherally in aesthetics. They do not explore aesthetics or make them into a separate issue, they simply create them. Nevertheless, they are not functionalists of the old school. On the contrary. They have understood very well that in Postmodernism it is not function that determines the form of an object, but that form is the actual meta-plane of design. It is much more satisfying for users and designers today to sit on a beautiful chair that is impressive in its construction and innovative in its choice of material than to sit on a chair that is superficially comfortable.

Myto is both a typical and an atypical Grcic product. Grcic, who has committed himself above all to new construction principles in recent years – his chair and table designs for Classicon constantly address folds, in order to move from the second to the third dimension, his designs for Magis or Moroso, Flos or Plank looked at skeleton-type structures that were also reminiscent of stealth bombers. Grcic, a fan of sports cars, has also looked over Lamborghini's shoulder. And somehow Myto looks like a logical continuation of these works. Myto is atypical because for the first time Grcic did not commit to the construction as the starting point for his thinking, but to a material – in order to achieve a particular effect in terms of statics – that could probably not admit any other appearance. But Grcic remains true to himself even in this unusual approach; he is the shining prototype of the inventor, even if others are close on his heels.

STEFAN DIEZ, who worked with Grcic for a time, operates in the same category for a good reason. But the material very often is the design starting point in his case. Diez throws himself into investigating materials, and is passionate about testing their boundaries. And from these explorations of how much load materials can take, he develops products whose formal language may look minimalist at a first glance, but which on closer examination show a refreshing charm deriving above all from the design of technical details.

Stefan Diez / Thonet 404

· ·

Diez's products are always coherent and multi-faceted in the best sense – a quality that can be found in only a few designers at this level of consistency. The wide variety of themes he addresses should also be emphasised. He designs furniture, tableware and bags, and also entire exhibitions. His clients include Rosenthal, Authentics, Wilkhahn, Elmar Flötotto, the Nymphenburg Porcelain Manufactory, Schönbuch and WMF. He recently designed a bentwood chair for Thonet, the Form 404. And in the context of the great names of Modernism he succeeded in wresting something new from both material and form, an innovative approach that nevertheless – and herein lies his strength – is able to fit in quite naturally with the existing bentwood classics.

Clemens Weisshaar takes a quite different line in finding form, or to put it better, in inventing form. He runs a design practise in Munich and Stockholm with his partner Reed Kram. He is interested above all in the possibilities of using digital technology to extend the range of construction and design. He takes on the role of a scientist, watching with fascination where technology is going, and almost by chance creates new looks for things and different results. Thanks to new computer technology, the jagged legs of the take Breeding Tables, dating from 2002, take on a different, unique form. Each item is a unique object, and nevertheless part of the product series that Moroso makes under the name Countach. In his My Private Sky edition for Nymphenburg, Weisshaar combines computer technology with traditional craft. The position of the constellations at the client's birth is calculated and then transferred to the plates by hand, using a porcelain painting technique that is thousands of years old. The complete edition of this extreme example of personal design is limited to 110 copies. As well as product design, Weisshaar puts a great deal of energy into designing spaces. Architecture and digital technology are mutually dependent in the 30-Year Anniversary show of the Permanent Collection installation for the Centre Georges Pompidou in Paris (2007) or in the master plan for exhibition architecture for the Design Annual fair in Frankfurt (2006). They fuse to form a single unit.

Something similar could be said about the New York Aranda/Lasch architecture practise. Benjamin Aranda and Christopher Lasch, both Columbia graduates, founded a joint practise in 2003. They are interested in interiors and above all

in furniture, as well as in architectural experiments. Like chemists, they develop their objects from the smallest molecules, arranging them in clumps and then fusing them together to make larger units. Their work too looks like a digital graphic translated into reality – except that this seems to have been created with the resources of classical model-making. Austria has given us Buchegger, Denoth, Feichtner, who run a product design and commu-

Thomas Feichtner / Axiome

nications practice. THOMAS FEICHTNER, who is responsible for the group's product design, has designed a whole series of folded objects. Door handles, chairs, indeed even a set of cutlery seem to have been produced by the same mathematical formula and look as though they have come directly from the NASA research lab. Feichtner understands the stealth camouflage aesthetic, transferred to all kinds of everyday things, also as a counter-strategy to commerce-based perception of design, something he rejects vehemently.

In contrast to this, the Dutch designer PIEKE BERGMANS is not interested in using design to camouflage an object, but in infecting existing objects with unrelated materials, typologies and forms. Even when she was still a student she covered Jasper Morrison's Rosenthal Moon service with so much adhesive tape that forms literally acquired a hump. At the time of writing, Bergmanns is working on an even

greater infection. In her Crystal Virus project hand-blown crystal glass meets tables and chairs – in the most accurate sense of the word. While it is being blown, the red-hot glass is pressed against the edge of a table or chair, and worked on further there. The two objects can do nothing other than interact: the crystal viruses adapt to their host's shape and the host permanently carries the scars of burning from the molten glass.

Pieke Bergmans / Vitra Virus

••

PATRICIA URQUIOLA is a Spaniard who lives in Italy. Linking materials and technologies innovatively has long fascinated her. To do this, she alternates between high technology and craft techniques – often for the same product. The transition from two to three dimensions is Urquiola's central interest as an architect. She often finds ideas for her wide range of designs in the actual production process. Take her Antibodi chair for Moroso: without further ado she announces that the actual left-hand side of the covering fabric, with its open seam addi-

tions like flowers, is the right-hand side, thus creating a new and hitherto unknown aesthetic. When developing her Landscape Service for Rosenthal, launched at Ambiente 2008 in Frankfurt, she laid various layers of porcelain one on top of the other like transparent films, thus creating fascinating effects with the contrast of closed and translucent parts for the individual elements. For her Tropicalia chair programme, presented by Moroso

Patricia Urquiola/Antibodi

at the 2008 Milan Furniture Fair, geometrical tubular steel frames were covered with woven polyester cords. The overlapping of the cords produces an austere woven texture that looks architectural, reminiscent of Mexican handicrafts.

The New York designer STEPHEN BURKS is also interested in the possibility of placing traditional craft techniques in a new context. The TaTu wire furniture collection, occasional tables in various sizes, always made up of a tray, a bowl and a basket – complemented by a single stool – was created using a traditional South African wire-weaving technology, though in the past this had been used only for small accessories and applied art products. Burks shifts this technique into a new dimension, thus also relieving it of the almost kitschy look it has in its usual context. The transformation achieved by Burks' design makes the technique and the material suddenly look polyglot and modern. And of course the manufacturer, Artecnica, has the collection produced in South Africa, where its technique originated. Burks experiments with cheap materials and traditional techniques for Cappellini as well. A series of tables and

Stephen Burks/Cappellini Love Small Table

stools called Love Collection has been created from shredded waste paper. This is a co-operative project between Cappellini and Burks, set up to develop ecological products. Burks has the individual paper strips, all the same width and length because they have been professionally shredded, placed in layers and glued by hand, so that it is possible to maintain creative control over the emerging patterns and colour combinations – in contrast with the usual papier mâché process – until the furniture is complete.

It is reassuring: inventors never tire of researching materials and techniques so that new forms can be created. They find it easier to achieve this – so it would seem – the fewer ideologies are twining themselves around design as a discipline. But it would not be correct to reduce them to the rank of formalists. The fact is that Postmodern society is entirely in a position to change itself and to develop further on the basis of a single new form.

PHILIP MICHAEL WOLFSON

1 Origami chair
In one of his important early works in the Origami series, using welded and folded sheet steel with an acid patinated finish, Wolfson explores abstraction through penetration, folding, layering and juxtaposition, creating what he calls "a visual aggression" that makes viewers take a longer, harder look at the piece.

2 Line Series
Part of a series of furniture that represents Wolfson's investigation of fluid motion, in this case beginning with a line.

3 Longevity desk – Shou 1
The form of this desk is an interpretation of the Chinese character, Shou, or Longevity. In the process of generating it in three dimensions, Wolfson began to question the actual decipherability of the character itself. Traditionally, 100 variations of Shou represent blessings and longevity, suggesting that 99 more variations (in both form and function) of the design could follow.

1

2

3

JULIAN MAYOR

1 General Dynamic armchair
   Mayor designed this faceted shell
   of a chair based on a representation of a 3D wave.

OSKAR ZIETA

2 The Lamp
   This prototype is a study in exquisitely creased sheet metal.

O-D-A

3 Sub stool
   The idea for this stackable stool
   began with the designers slitting
   and folding paper. This model was
   then transferred into aluminum
   sheet by cutting and welding the
   parts together.

1

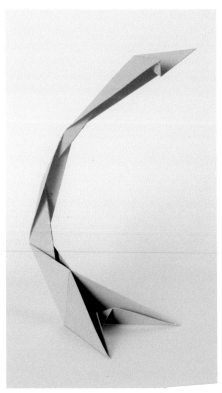

2

3

....

STEFAN DIEZ
1   Thonet 404 chair

BIHAIN
Michaël Bihain
2   Mosquito chair
This stackable chair is made from a
leaf of waisted wood and may be piled
up in two ways, either vertically, for
the pragmatists, or diagonally, for those
who want a more graphical look.

1

2

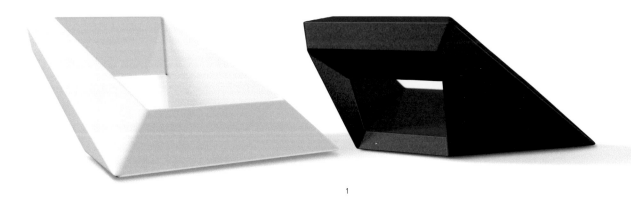

1

**THOMAS FEICHTNER /BUCHEGGER,
DENOTH, FEICHTNER**
Thomas Feichtner

1 Public chair
A chair for use in public spaces, the
unusual form of which invites use.

2 Topless chair
It lacks a backrest, but is no bar stool.

3 Table chair
This wood and chrome occasional table
opens to reveal a seat. Users must
interact with the design to discern its
second function.

4 Eyry lamp
Eyry, with a wing span of 1.4 metres,
has a fabric-covered wire frame that
allows light to diffuse through it in all
directions. The textile "jacket" can be
easily detached and varied, creating a
different look and feel in an interior
with each.

5 FSB 5930 door handle
5930 disobeys the rules of ergonom-
ics, breaks with axial orientation – and
functions beautifully nonetheless.

6 Water bottle
7 Bric drinking glass

8 Cutt cutlery
Neither function nor ergonomic suit-
ability determined the form of this set
of eating utensils, yet no one can resist
the desire to use it.

2

3

6

7

4

5

8

**THOMAS FEICHTNER /BUCHEGGER,
DENOTH, FEICHTNER**
Thomas Feichtner

1 Honey chair
The question was: can a chair (made
for greater comfort) assume the characteristics of a stool (made for greater
range of motion)? Honey is a chair that
does both, and with a creased geometric beauty.

2 Coma desk lamp
The self-supporting metal enclosure is
made all in one piece. Coma was designed as a lamp for drawing: the light,
just above the tabletop, focuses the
artist"s concentration on the paper.

3 FX10 lounge chair
Again, a sharp-edged seat that is nonetheless comfortable. Feichtner thought
of FX10's sections as similar to the
blocks of ice used in the construction
of an igloo.

1

2

3

THOMAS FEICHTNER/BUCHEGGER, DENOTH, FEICHTNER
Thomas Feichtner
1 Axiome chair
A chair that eschews the familiar organic forms that typically invite one to take a seat, Axiome challenges the notion that form follows function. In faceted powder-coated aluminium sheet, the chair reveals its comfort only when used.

MATHIAS BENGTSSON
2,3 MAC chair
The Modular Aluminium Concept chair comprises 34 modular sections of extruded white powder-coated aluminium.

1

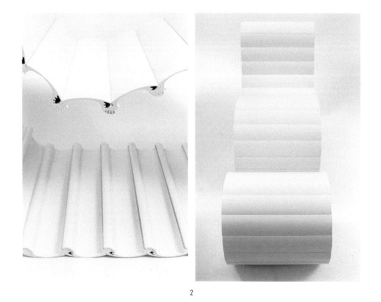

2

3

1

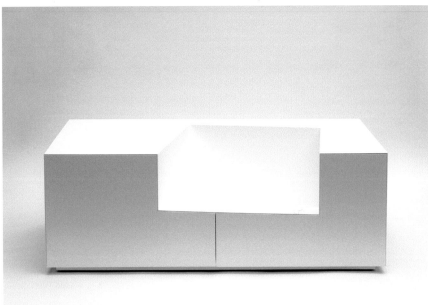

2

3

ALEXANDER KNELLER
1   Side Chair One
2   Side Chair Two
    A pair of furniture units that multi-task, combining seating, tabletop and storage.

FOR USE
3   Twist table
    These Romanian designers rotated elements of this table 90° from top to bottom, giving the whole table the appearance of twisting slightly around its vertical axis.

PHILIP MICHAEL WOLFSON
4   LineDesk
    The LINE series illustrates Wolfson's fascination with walking the thin line between making sculptural objects and making objects that function – seeing just how far he can push form and physics.

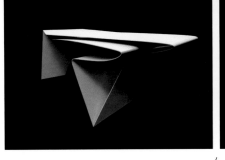
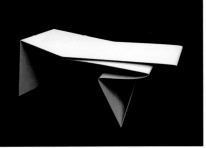

4

DAVE KEUNE
Stealth chair
The classic lines of its upholstery and integrated cushioning contrast with Stealth's futuristic metal body and swivel base.

THOMAS FEICHTNER /BUCHEGGER, DENOTH, FEICHTNER
Thomas Feichtner
1   Two Axiomes in Rotation glasses
These two drinking glasses began with Feichtner's signature geometric forms but, for the first time, do not consist of straight surfaces. The pieces come from a root form that achieves its rounded three-dimensional form by being rotated around its axis and, finally, by being reflected horizontally, creating two different glasses from one form. The black appearance of the dark glass is achieved by combining multicoloured glass so that, if backlit, red, blue and violet shades appear.

JEAN MARIE MASSAUD
2   Terminal 1 armchair

1

2

3

4

DICKENS&WILSON
Anthony Dickens
3   Origami cafe chair
Wilson devised a system to connect three legs in such a way that the load they supported tightened the joints connecting the legs, requiring no screws, bolts, pegs, fixings or tools. The legs come apart easily for storage and reassembly and flat-pack easily for transport and retailing. The tables are made from three identical flat-pressed steel legs that slot together to create the tripod base. Each leg features two slots, positioned on a different three-point plane. The interlocking design is a unique, patented system.

BRAM BOO
4   White Nun chair
Designed for the art and design studio Z33, which is situated in an old beguinage in Hasselt, Belgium. The shape of the chair was inspired by the capes of the nuns who lived there.

ANTHONY DICKENS

1 Anglpoise Fifty table light
Dickens' inspiration came from the
original Anglepoise® lamp invented in
1932. The designer set this lamp at an
angle of 50 degrees (which efficiently
lights both desktop and the workspace
as a whole) and then cast it like an
archeological relic. "In simple terms,"
Dickens says, "it's the cheeky kid
brother snapping at the heels of his
older sibling."

2 Around Clock timepiece
Dickens wanted to represent time in a
more intuitive way than a traditional
clock. Peoples' sense of time is created
by the rotation of the earth into and
out of sunlight, so the cylindrical body
of his Around Clock rotates past the
static red time line so that users simultaneously see the present slipping into
the past and the future approaching.
The name "Around Clock" derives from
Dickens' belief that there is rarely a
need to represent minutes in anything
smaller than 15-minute increments.

RICCARDO BLUMER
WITH MATTEO BORGHI

3 Ghisa outdoor seating
This modular outdoor seating system
is made from lamellar cast iron and is
highly adaptable. Mirror-image modules
create straight seating with alternating
backs, semi-circular, circular or wave-
shape compositions.

1

2

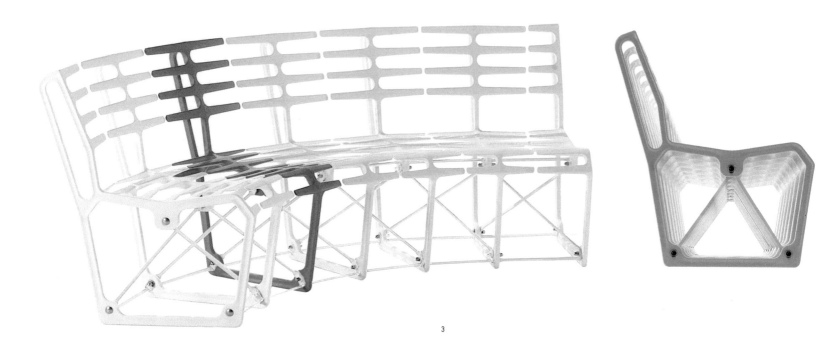

3

TAKESHI MIYAKAWA

1,3 3x3 chair
This geometric chair is composed of three triangular elements cut in different angles to emphasise perspective distortion.

2 Wedge table
An angular table composed of several faceted surfaces to achieve minimum thickness but maximum strength.

DEFDEF.
Anna Blattert, Daniel Gafner, Thilo Fuente

4 Unité de Vernissage stool /table
Originally designed for the opening of Platform'08, an art exhibition in Zürich, Unité can act as stool, lounge table or bar-height table, depending on how the shell is mounted atop the "tree" base.

1

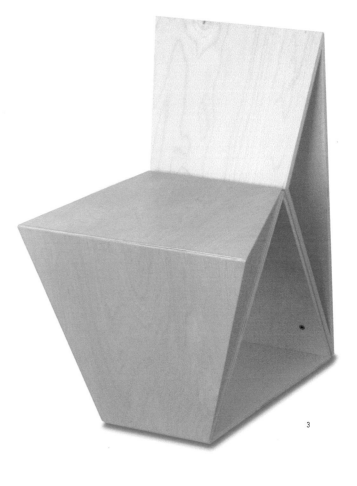

3

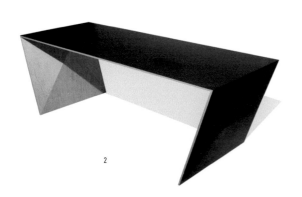

2

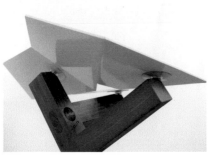

4

RAW EDGES
Shay Alkalay & Yael Mer
Page 98

Shay Alkalay has been known to be a bit untidy, shall we say, leaving drawers and doors open when rushing headlong out of the house each morning. Hence, his headlining 2008 storage element, Stack, for Established & Sons. Usually a chest of drawers relies on an exterior frame, back panel and runners that correspond to each drawer, meaning that height is determined by the frame and drawers open in a single direction only. With Stack, Alkalay reinvents the drawer mechanism, trading out the external frame for a hidden internal structure, which makes drawer height independent of the frame and allows each to open in two directions. Stack concedes to the idea of organisation (it is a set of drawers, after all) while giving a naughty nod to chaos. This attention to a tool of organisation in a way that looks – but isn't – precarious is revisited in Alkalay's Pivot cabinet for Arco. A bipedal cabinet that leans against the wall, Pivot contains three drawers that can be pulled out simultaneously because they are hinged.

This supremely practical impracticality seems to be a signature of Alkalay and partner Yael Mer's London studio, Raw Edges. The 32-year-old Israelis met at design school in Jerusalem before moving to London to attend the Royal College of Art. Today, not immune to the headless children's toy trend going around, the pair has dreamed up the Bin Bag Bear, a trash bag shaped like a guillotined teddy bear. Stickystains are iron-on graphics that conceal unsightly blotches on clothing (again, the tidiness theme). As the name suggests, their Rocking Slippers embed felt slippers into a low-slung rocking chair. The wall-mounted, doughnut-shaped Flying Fish Bowl revolves, keeping your goldfish ... dizzy. Raw Edges milk cartons indicate fat content by shape instead of colour: slender cartons for skim and cartons of a certain girth for whole milk.

This year's Tailored stools, made from paper and polyurethane foam, come in an edition of 48 and are generated on a custom basis by creating a sartorial pattern for each client, according to their dimensions. Just for the record, Mer is a petite stool; Alkalay, tall and narrow.

1

RAW-EDGES
Shay Alkalay

1,3 **Stack chest of drewers**
Usually a chest of drawers consists of an exterior frame, back panel and runners on each drawer. The height is limited to the size of the frame and the drawer can only be opened in one direction. Alkalay challenges these conventions with his multicoloured, "floating" drawer units that can be stacked to various heights and pushed and pulled open in both directions. As sculptural as it is practical, Stack comes in two sizes together in two multicolour colourways.

2 **Pivot drawers**
This solid wood cabinet is built on tall legs and features two drawers that can hinge, making it possible to open both at the same time, something impossible with a conventional set of drawers.

2

3

BAS VAN DER VEER

1 Paper table
A small coffee table, demonstrating the strength of paper in combination with mathematical models.

JASON MILLER

2 I Was Here table series
I Was Here is a series of tables made from "graffiti-proof," recycled, plastic wood inscribed with actual graffiti culled from New York City's tabletops and park benches.

PAUL LOEBACH

3 Step stools
Inspired by the simple versatility of American Shaker furniture, this nesting set of stools in three shades of green pull out to form a set of steps.

ECAL/RAPHAËL VON ALLMEN

4 Gum Tab outdoor stool
Rub Tan, an outdoor material used mainly on sport fields and playgrounds, has been made into a stool that is formed in a flat mould and then stretched on a rigid steel structure to receive its shape.

CORDULA KEHRER

5 Oona table/storage
Small items, books and magazines can be placed on the surfaces of this bedside table.

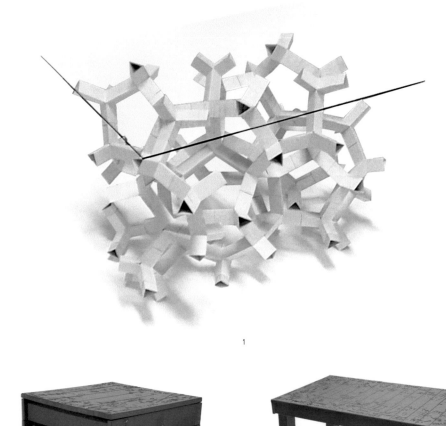

1

2

3

4
5

READYMADE PROJECTS
Stephen Burks
Cappellini Love bowl & vases
The Cappellini Love collection is the
company's ecoconscious label created by
Giulio Cappellini in collaboration with
Stephen Burks. The first products included
these silicone and mosaic tile bowls hand-
made using a proprietary process developed by Burks in a women's community
centre in South Africa.

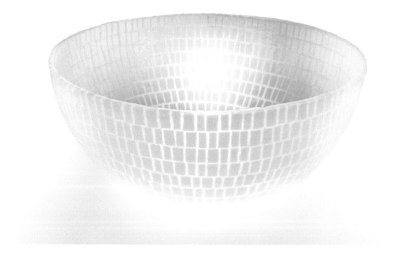

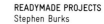

READYMADE PROJECTS
Stephen Burks
Cappellini Love tables
Some of the first products chosen for inclusion in the Cappellini Love ecoconscious collection were triangular tables made from shredded recycled magazines and a non-toxic hardener. Like papier mâché, the technique of layering the paper strips by hand allows great variation in density, colour and pattern. The production was outsourced to artisan groups in South Africa.

ADRIEN ROVERO
Particule stool
With the assistance of VIA and borrowing the industrial technology used to make loading pallets, Rovero made a stool from compressed and moulded wood chips (their volume reduced to a quarter of real size). All three legs are made using the same mould, which facilitates mass production and enables delivery in parts. Adhesion of the chips is ensured by a natural adhesive made from tannin, a substance extracted from the bark of certain trees.

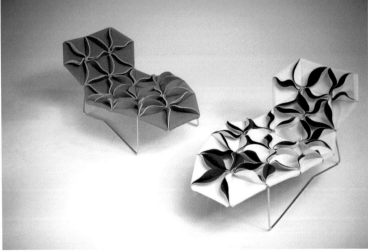

PATRICIA URQUIOLA
Antibodi chaise longue
Antibodi is a non-upholstered lounge chair decorated with sewn triangular blossoms which have lightly padded petals and are made to be reversible in felt and wool fabric / wool fabric and leather. With the petals face up, the chair looks exuberant, face down it looks exuberantly quilted.

The bad news: wood exudes pentachlorophenol, paint gives off the carcinogen trichloroethylene. Plastic, glues, insulation and even domestic cleaning products emit formaldehyde. Every product emits toxins for several years following its manufacture. The good news? Mathieu Lehanneur's product designs can improve the quality of your air and water while raising the bar on the aesthetics of sustainable design. But that's not all, the Paris-based designer also finds a myriad ways to bring nature (the idea and the object) back into our everyday lives. Even though a number of these objects are only at the prototype stage, they challenge previously imagined limits of green design, as well as the unspoken limits of designers as problem solvers. We can do better than we have and Lehanneur has proved it.

In 2008, Lehanneur won the Best Invention Award for his prototype air purifier, Bel-Air, designed the year before for the Paris art/design/science gallery, Le Laboratoire. With scientist David Edwards, Lehanneur made Bel-Air, as he calls it, "a domestic spacecraft," which, like every good NASA craft, filters out ambient poisons. Bel-Air is a living filter that draws air in and absorbs contaminants by using plants – gerbera, philodendron, spathiphyllum, pathos or chlorophytum – selected for their capacity to filter out the icky stuff through their leaves and roots.

Lehanneur, who was born in 1974 in Rochefort, France, graduated from ENSCI-Les Ateliers in 2001 and immediately established his own studio, collaborated with Anthony van den Bossche to create Local River for the New York Artists Space Gallery. Local River, a blown and thermoformed glass tank, serves as a storage unit for live freshwater fish combined with a tiny vegetable patch for those who want to eat locally in order to reduce their environmental footprint. While the plants pull nutrients from the nitrate-rich waste of the fish, they purify the water in which the fish live. Lehanneur's goal is for Local River to replace the ornamental aquarium with a "refrigerator-aquarium." This may prove additional good news: midnight raids on the fridge should become a bit more complicated.

MATHIEU LEHANNEUR & DAVID EDWARDS (SCIENTIST)
Bel-Air air filter
Bel-Air is a live filter that absorbs contaminants in the air through the roots and leaves of plants and greenery selected for their filtering capacity, including the gerbera, the philodendron, the spathiphyllum, the pathos and the chlorophytum.

MATHIEU LEHANNEUR & ANTHONY VAN DEN BOSSCHE (SPIN DOCTOR)
Local River fish and vegetable farm
The Locavores appeared in San Francisco in 2005, defining themselves as a group of culinary adventurers who eat foods produced within a radius of 100 miles (160 km) of their city. By doing so, they aimed to reduce their impact on the environment. The idea quickly rippled outward from the Bay Area. Local River is a fish farm and kitchen garden in one. While the plants extract nutrients from the nitrate-rich waste of the fish, they act as a natural filter that purifies the water and maintains a vital balance for the eco-system in which the fish live. The same technique is used on large-scale pioneer aquaponics/fish-farms that raise tilapia.

1,2 Bel-Air air filter

1

2

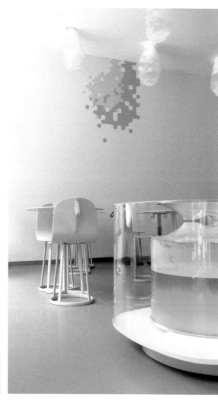

MATHIEU LEHANNEUR
Flood restaurant furniture
Lehanneur placed an aquarium in the centre of each section of the restaurant, containing over 100 litres of micro-algae. By photosynthesis, the algae produces pure oxygen. The designer also applied the "flooding" theme to his furniture by dip-coating chairs and tables in PVC. To underscore the modified, oxygen-enriched air, he created large blown glass lamps.

1

DESIGN VIRUS
PIEKE BERGMANS

1 Light Blubs lamps
Bergmans explains that a Light Blub "is a light bulb that has gone way out of line. Infected by the dreaded Design Virus, these Blubs have taken on all kinds of forms and sizes you wouldn't expect from such well behaving and reliable little products." This series of lamps are all unique handcrafted crystal pieces, equipped with LEDs by Solid Lighting Design. They continue Bergmans focus on mass customisation and "Perfect Imperfection."

2 Crystal Virus vases
A series of virus-formed crystal vases made by hand at Royal Leerdam Crystal Holland. Large, heated crystal bubbles are pressed onto wooden furniture and while the crystal burns into the wood, some of the wood's texture is integrated into the vase. Bergmans then displays vase and furniture together as an installation.

3 Crystal Virus – Space Invaders vases
Bergmans' Space Invaders crystal vases stand alone, without being coupled with other pieces of furniture. Now consumers can choose which furniture elements, interiors or architecture will be infected by the Crystal Virus themselves. The massive size of these vases pushed the limits of crystal blowing.

4 Vitra Virus vases
The Crystal Virus, now in a fierce red, infects famous pieces by Charles & Ray Eames, Maarten van Severen, Sori Yanagi, Ronan & Erwan Bouroullec, Jean Prouvé and Jasper Morrison.

2

3

4

DRIFT
Ralph Nauta & Lonneke Gordijn
Pages 108–109, 186

The first object that designers – and lovers – Ralph Nauta and Lonneke Gordijn of Eindhoven-based DRIFT created together in 2006 was, appropriately, a loveseat. But the Water Web bench isn't your grandmother's loveseat. The bench, made from expanded polystyrene and polyurea, contains an operational water fountain. Intended for outdoor or indoor use, water is pumped through the bench until it spouts through a hole in the seat and then streams back into the bench through a mill-cut pattern in its surface.

DRIFT's work is as romantic and inventive as its designers. In 2007, their Dandelights synthesised nature and electronics. The power generated by a nine-volt battery nourishes actual dandelion seeds connected to it via a phosphorous bronze "stem," making the seeds grow and illuminating the LED lights inside the flowers.

A related light sculpture called Fragile Future, which won a Lights of the Future award from the German Design Council in 2008, uses the same materials to construct a modular installation that appears to grow like ivy over a wall. The construction is programmed, using distance-sensors and a computer chip, to "protect" itself if someone comes too close, by feigning disrepair.

But it's Ghost that has garnered the couple the most attention. Produced between 2007 and 2008, the seating collection consists of eight dining chairs, two armchairs (King and Queen) and one stool inspired by the days of monarchy when a ruler granting his subjects an audience was the only one allowed to take a seat. In those times, the shape of a chair was an indication of a person's social position and only the king and queen enjoyed the luxury of armrests. The body of the rectilinear Ghost chairs are transparent but each contains a milky, spectral image generated inside the Plexi by a laser. Those who don't already have a ghost in residence should perhaps consider acquiring one.

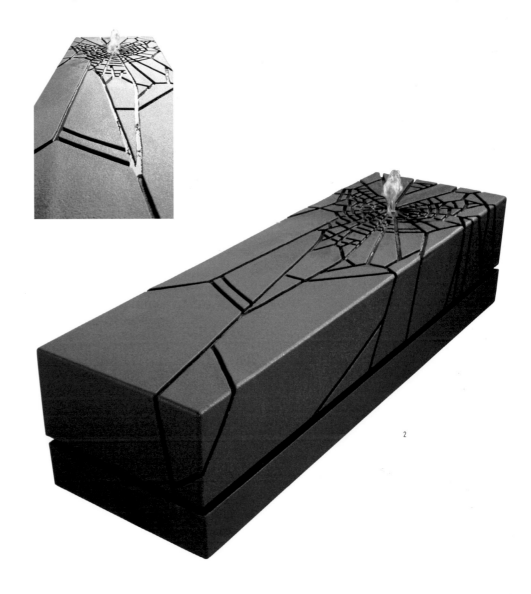

2

1,3 Ghost Collection seating
The collection includes eight dining chairs, two armchairs (the Queen and the King) and one stool, all laser-etched with an abstract sheer image, an "inner ghost."

2 Water Web bench
This sofa for outside and inside use came into being as an unusual version of the loveseat. Water is pumped up from inside the bench through the seat and flows via the mill-cut pattern back into the body of the sofa. In the sun, the sparkling water contrasts with the matt finish of the bench. Water Web comes in three patterns and three colours.

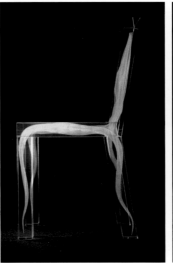

3

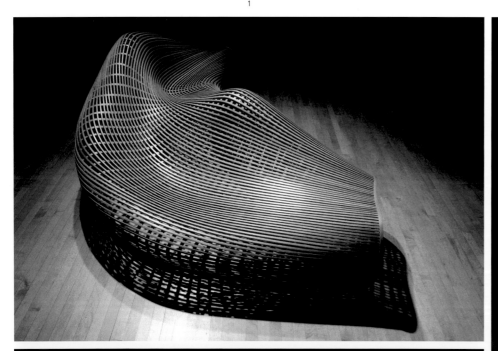

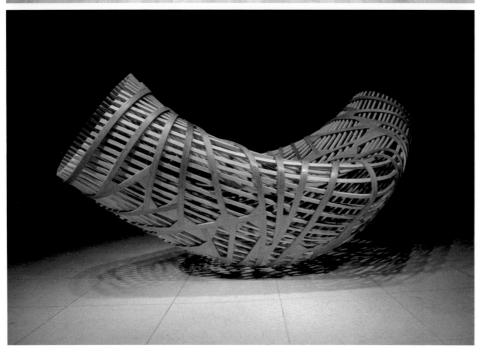

MATTHIAS-STUDIO
Matthias Pliessnig

1–3 Providence bench
Several compound curves, which echo the human body, collide and flow in this piece, giving Providence structural strength and sensual lines. Flowing water and flowing wind, as well as boat building, were Pliessnig's influences.

4 Point bench
This piece explores the idea of inside/outside by exposing the structure that holds the form together. Point touches the floor at one point, demanding that users constantly keep their balance as the form shifts beneath them in multiple directions.

2

5-7 Waive bench

In 2006, Pliessnig built and sailed a boat constructed from a fabric-covered frame made from wood strips. Waive is based on the designer's boat-building and sailing adventure. Pliessnig believes that wood can be a dynamic material and wants people to question their notion of what wood is and what furniture is. "Furniture should respond to people," he says. "I thought of Waive as a soft grid of wood being formed by the sitter's weight. In essence, I am making furniture that resembles the flexibility of plastic using the ancient material of wood."

6
7

CARL OJERSTAM

1 Turbinella lampshade
Ojerstam worked with Materialise.MGX to produce his 3D-printed lampshade.

TOMITADESIGN

Tomita Kazuhiko

2 Banana chaise with ottoman
Woven in double layers of fine rattan, this seating allows modular cushions in handwoven fabrics to pass smoothly through apertures in the surface to stay folded against the seat and backrest under the weight of a sitter.

3 Su Su Su armchair
Achieving a corpulent appearance and comfort without revealing this seat's structure requires the finest hand-weaving.

1

2

3

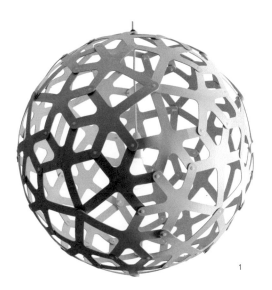

1

2

DAVID TRUBRIDGE

1 Coral lampshade
A hanging pendant lampshade based on classic polyhedron geometry and made from sustainably produced plywood.

MARK BRAUN

2 Kluwen seating
These benches made from smoked oak and ash wood make any room a playground.

3

DAVID TRUBRIDGE

3 Sprial Islands benches
Spiral Islands was inspired by the many small Pacific Islands, which all have identical clouds floating above them.

4 Suncorp bench
This seating was made from steam-bent American ash and plywood.

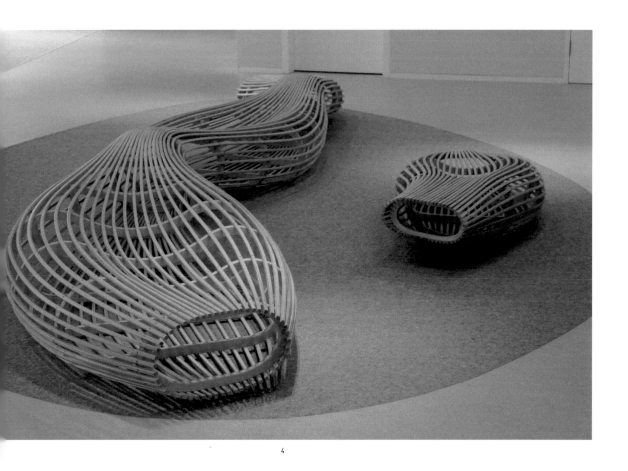

4

MATHIAS BENGTSSON

1 Spun chair
A chair made from a fibre tow-on line impregnated with resin and passed between two rotating discs as it is moved by a 6-axis robot arm. Together the discs spin approximately 50 meters of carbon-fibre.

2 Spun lounge chair
The featherweight, semi-transparent structure of the Spun carbon-fibre lounge chair belies the strength of the carbon.

3 Slice lounge chair
This seat was made from 99 individual layers.

5 Slice chair
First drawn by hand and later modelled in clay, the Slice chair combines organic shapes with cutting-edge technology. Slice is constructed as an assemblage of horizontal cross-sections that stack into a uniquely lateral profile.

JULIAN MAYOR

4 Clone chair
Mayor "cloned" this piece in CNC-milled plywood from plans of a Queen Anne chair found in New York's Metropolitan Museum.

1

3

4

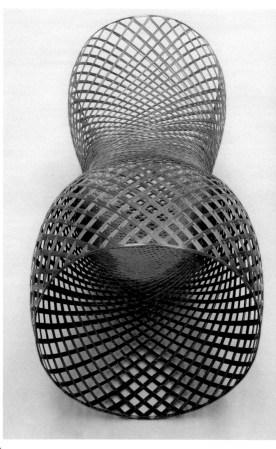

2

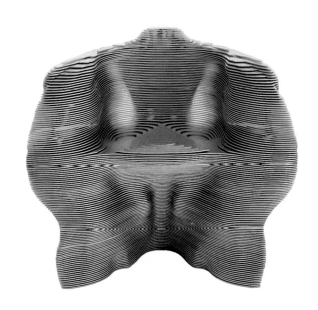
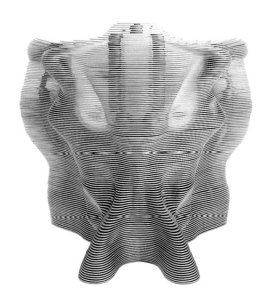

5

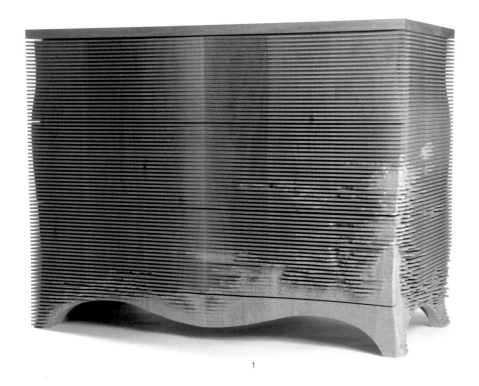

GARETH NEAL

1 George chest of drawers
Contained within this contemporary rectilinear oak chest of drawers is the ghost
of its past, a 1780 George III commode,
as if through the erosion of time its past
form has begun to be revealed.

2 Capillary table

3,4 Anne side table
Contained within this contemporary
side table is the ghost of its past, a 1730
Queen Anne side table.

JULIAN MAYOR

5 Empress chair
Although based on a human seat, the
Empress chair was designed in San
Francisco and its form is also intended
to represent a skyline.

2

3

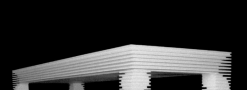

4

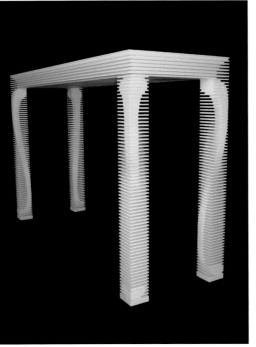

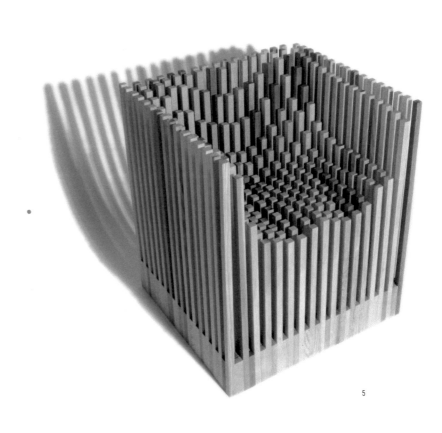

5

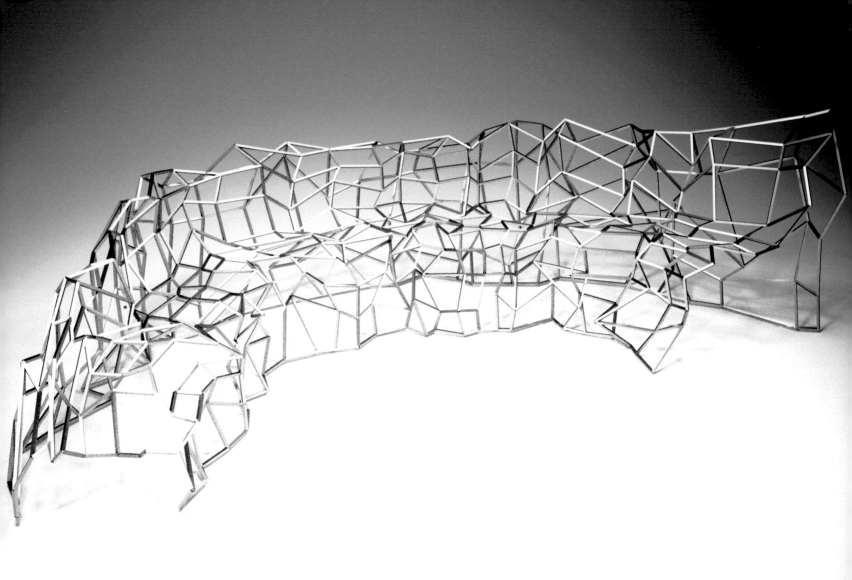

1

JULIAN MAYOR
1 Burnout bench
The form of the Burnout bench is based on a sculptural wave described in 3D by a computer. It is realised as a series of five individual seats that fit together.

STEVEN HOLL ARCHITECTS
Steven Holl and Nick Gelpi
2 Porosity bench
A seat that can be seen through and which casts shadows and complex patterns of light.

2

MAX LAMB
Hexagonal pewter stool
Lamb carved a negative mould directly into the wet sand on a beach and then filled it with molten pewter. Once cool, he removed the sand to leave a solid pewter stool.

1

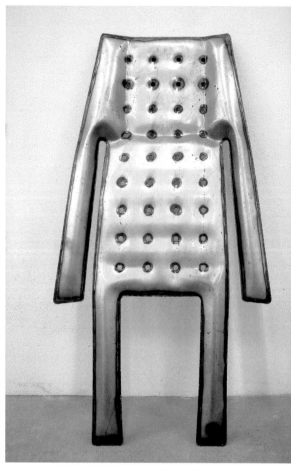

2

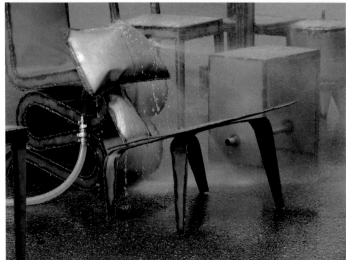

6
7

Pages 86, 120–121

OSKAR ZIETA

Polish architect (1975) Oskar Zieta's material of choice is sheet metal – inflated sheet metal, that is. The designer's Plopp stool has the appearance of a blow-up raft one might find floating in a swimming pool, but weighs a couple of kilos and, despite its lightweight, squishy look, is perfectly rigid and stable. Teaching at the faculty of the ETH Zürich, Zieta has positioned Plopp as the flagship of two years of trial-and-error innovation – and has repositioned sheet metal altogether.

Zieta made Plopp using Free Internal Pressure Deformation (FIDU), a modification of tube hydroforming, a method used in auto production, but never to create furniture. Plopp's outline was sheared out of a metal sheet (chromium nickel, aluminum, steel or various alloys) in duplicate and welded together with a flatbed laser. Zieta then injected high-pressure water (3 - 50 bar) between the two sheets to force them into a 3D form. Zieta also used this method to create his tufted-looking Plopp chair, although today he uses air instead of water.

When he was unable to find a manufacturer, Zieta built his own factory in Poland where FIDU allows him to create more complex deformations of the material, which means that his furniture can be easily mass-customised at low cost using well established techniques and machinery. Best of all, each piece looks expressive, almost hand-made – or blown up by a pair of human lungs.

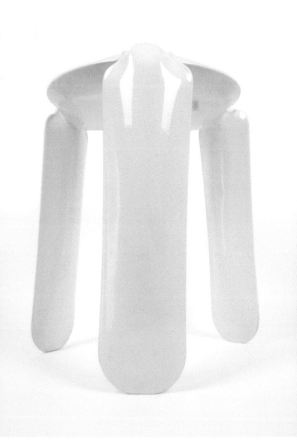

3

4

5

1,6 Plopp chair
2   Plopp prototype
3   Plopp stool (inox polished)
4   Plopp stool
5   Plopp stool
8   DMY Berlin Ausstellung
    Zieta created stable furniture from
    thin metal sheets using CNC machines
    and hydroformed metal surfaces and
    creating 3D-volumes from 2D-sheets.
    After cutting out two copies of each
    piece, he welded these together and
    injected high pressure water or air to
    make the flat pattern swell into three
    dimensions, like a blow-up pool raft.
    The result is a light construction that
    can be easily mass-customised at low
    cost using well-established techniques.

7   Aufgeblasene Designer
    The last module of the annual MAS
    course at Zürich's ETH focused on digit-
    ally processing sheet metal. The goal
    was to teach students how to work with
    a laser-cutter, bending machine and
    welding unit. Using the "hydro-forming
    process" developed by CAAD member
    Oskar Zieta, students made their own
    versions of classic pieces of furniture by
    Eames and Gehry, for instance.

8

MAX LAMB

A product designer who exults in dominating his materials – carving, moulding, smelting, chiseling, turning – as well as discovering unusual technical means to do so, British designer Max Lamb weds industrial production and hand craftsmanship to great effect.

Born in Cornwall in 1980, Lamb currently lives and works in London. During college, the designer carved a stool out of a solid block of polystyrene, a series he would continue (strengthening the pieces by coating them with polyurethane rubber) during his master's programme at the Royal College of Art. He produced his Poly Chair in 2006, along with a number of rugged yet featherweight tables, stools, dining chairs and armchairs. To make his Hexagonal Pewter stool the same year, he poured molten pewter into a mould cut into the wet black sand of a South Cornish beach. A banner year for experimentation, 2006 also saw his use of foam made from potato starch to extrude long thick noodles that he then coaxed into the form of a lounge chair. The Starch Chair was intended for use in a summer garden where it could be left to compost in the autumn.

Much of Lamb's work starts with materials and manufacturing research but he looks into methods both sophisticated and crude. In 2007 he carved his Ladycross Sandstone Chair out of a block of quarried sandstone. The next year, he took up expanded polystyrene again, handcarving the EPS but then casting it in bronze for the New York-based Johnson Trading Gallery. During the 2008 Art Basel design fair, Lamb mounted 18 lightweight concrete building blocks onto a woodturning lathe and turned them by hand to make stools. He had been named one of the fair's Designers of the Future. Indeed he is.

1 Poly furniture
2 Poly armchair
5 Poly dining table
6 Poly armchair
7 Poly dining chair
    Lamb carved a unique chair by hand
    from a block of expanded polystyrene
    and then coated it in a fast-drying
    poyurethane rubber spray.

3,4 Bronze Poly chair
    Lamb hand-carved a series of chairs
    from expanded polystyrene and then
    "lost-foam" cast them in bronze.

8,9 Solids of Revolution exhibition
    Lightweight concrete building blocks
    were turned by hand on a woodwork-
    ing lathe to create stools for the
    Designer of the Future show at Art
    Basel/Design Miami in 2008.

10 Solids of Revolution – felt stools
    The designer cut high-density wool
    felt into discs of varying diameter
    and then machined customised edge
    profiles into each. He then laminated
    the discs together to create nine dif-
    ferent stools.

11 Solids of Revolution – concrete stools
    Lamb individually mounted lightweight
    concrete building blocks onto a wood-
    turning lathe and turned them by hand
    to create individual concrete stools us-
    ing traditional woodworking tools.

1

2

3

4

6

7

8

9

10

11

Call him Mr. Mix-and-Match. Singapore-born, London-based Hunn Wai graduated from the Design Academy Eindhoven in the Netherlands in 2007, where he fell under the influence of Droog Design co-founder Gijs Bakker. A touch of Droog's experimentation, its sophisticated take on handicraft and its clever collisions of meaning and form are conspicuous in Wai's work.

The year of his graduation, Wai produced a family of chairs called Tre di Una made from a deliberately crude grafting of pigmented plastic clay onto generic beech and steel seating. The series emphasises the dichotomy between natural and synthetic materials, as well as machined and hand-made elements. Seemingly on the point of collapse, the seats are actually quite stable, but the wobbly looking bits are highlighted both by the more sober sections of traditional chair and by the playfully bright colors of clay and its patently childish workmanship. It is exactly this aesthetic of assemblage that renews both elements.

Again in 2007, Wai created the Readymade-like Sir Smith table by repurposing a second-hand dining table using steel, lace and acrylic paint. Wai compares his process to ripping MP3's from purchased CD's, again grafting details from his prized possessions onto flea market finds. Wai is interested in questioning what customers actually own when they purchase products, but what may be more interesting to ask is: what are the raw materials of the 21st century?

Along with the material implications suggested by the collage aesthetic, new forms of "craftsmanship" are also suggested by Wai's work. His 2008 Wood x Plastic shelf consists of sheets of smoke-coloured acrylic glass impaled on beech poles. The designer, however, went to great pains to fit the pieces together: after punching small holes in acrylic sheets, Wai heated the area around them precisely, pushed the poles through, sheet by sheet, and then allowed the plastic to cool and contract tightly around them – creating a fresh take on joinery.

Tre di Una chairs
Meaning "three from one," Tre di Una is a family of chairs created with the components of a generic wooden seat and plastic clay.

Twenty-four-year old Anna ter Haar's small and eclectic body of work moves easily between photography and video, product and furniture design, painting, fashion and performance art. It is held together by the coherence of her highly conceptual investigations, if not a single aesthetic.

Ter Haar plays with perceptions by projecting images onto people's bodies as in the 2007 thesis project for her Design Academy Eindhovan graduation, as well as an earlier video project about a body dysmorphic disorder entitled Verlopen. In Outlines, she created shelving and seating – partly drawn on the wall and partly built out – that existed between two and three dimensions. A vase made of packed soil that blooms to become a flower and, when the flower dies, returns to being merely a vase can't accomplish both tasks at once.

A one-time intern for Belgian fashion designer Raf Simons, ter Haar also produces conceptual garments. In 2006, Pump up the Volume, was a towering architectural version of outerwear covering the chest and rising above both shoulders in interlocking black planes. After studying the traditional dress of Estonia, Finland and the Netherlands, ter Haar created a contemporary synthesis in the form of a baroquely pleated dress. On spring 2008 catwalks, Dutch fashion label Klavers van Engelen used black, Gothic, ter Haar-designed sunglasses with frames that dripped down the models' faces.

This dripping of the plastic frames followed from ter Haar's previous academic experiments with cast polyurethane resin. The Buitenbeentje (Dutch for "odd man out") project, the designer explains, is a result of her fascination with the abnormal and the ugly. Ter Haar grafts one leg made of poured, dripping coloured resin onto otherwise conventional-looking stools, tables and chairs which, while appearing fluid, can still bear weight. She uses multiple shades of resin and sometimes allows a leg to flow upward. At other times, a cluster of slender drips will perform the work of a single, thicker leg. It should be interesting, in the near future, to see which discipline first claims ter Haar as its own.

Buitenbeentje furniture
Meaning "odd man out" in Dutch, these pieces with legs made of cast polyurethane resin represent movement congealed in material. They may look fluid but are strong enough to carry weight.

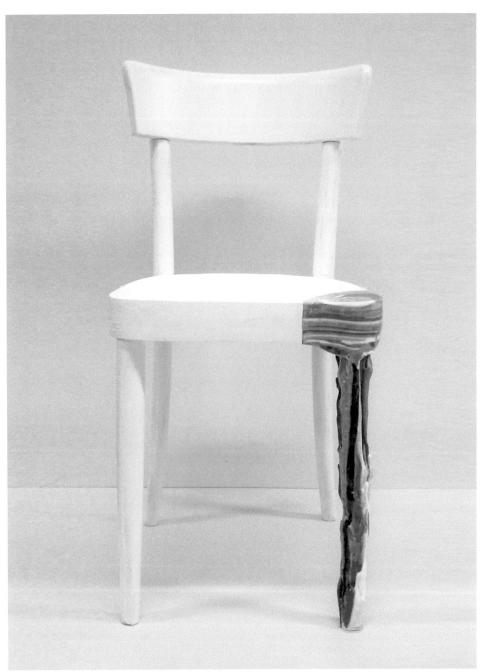

MAARTEN BAAS
1 Clay furniture
2,3 Chromed Clay furniture
All of Baas' Clay pieces are modelled by
hand and are therefore unique.

1

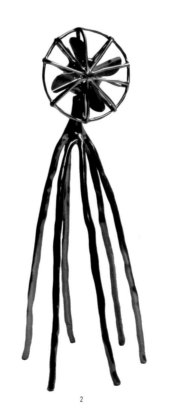

2

3

CRIS BARTELS

1. Skinterior No.9
2. Skinterior No.1
3. Skinterior No.4
4. Skinterior No.5
5. Skinterior No.7
6. Skinterior No.3
7. Skinterior No.2

To create a series of furniture inspired by slender models wearing couture, whose fragile frames are dominated by the garments, Bartels used a textile mould to generate its shapes. The structural material of the furniture (plastic) became secondary to the upholster, resulting in a seemingly clumsy shape that is not only very strong but also "vulnerably elegant" as Bartels phrases it.

STUDIO LIBERTINY
Tomáš Gabzdil Libertiny

8. Welded No.1 stool

Through the Welded project Libertiny experimented with the idea of repetition as a valuable process in manufacturing and the idea of using welding, designed for joining materials, to build a complete structure. In other words, he used a welding solder as building material and a welding machine as his tool. The objects were made by hand by soldering small bits, one by one, patiently waiting for the last layer to cool down before adding the next. Because weld itself is much stronger than the metal that it connects, the welded low stool is completely functional.

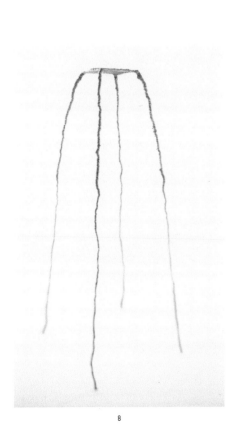

8

1

2

3

4

5

6

7

THE BENCH

1

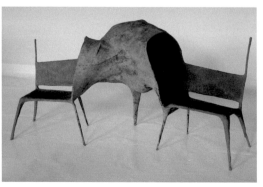

2

3

4

NACHO CARBONELL
1,2,4 Evolution bench
3 Soft Concrete bench

129

1

STUDIO LIBERTINY
Tomáš Gabzdil Libertiny
1   The Honeycomb Vase
2   The Beeswax Amphora

Libertiny's "collaboration" with honey bees pushes the boundaries of so-called conventional design by defying mass production and enabling nature to create what would normally be considered a man-made product. The vase's material derives from flowers as a by-product of bees and, in the form of a vase, ends up serving flowers on their last journey. It took 40,000 bees and one week to make a single vase. Without irony, Libertiny calls this process "slow prototyping."

2

JULIA LOHMANN
Resilience coffee and dining tables

As an Art Basel/Design Miami "Designer of the Future", Lohmann was asked to design objects made from both concrete and wool. Combining the two, she designed a pair of concrete and wool tables that play with a role reversal of the qualities associated with manmade and natural materials. She cast concrete, which is normally considered a structural and long-lasting material, in two-dimensional forms onto a woven wool backing. Then, in a design process that harnessed destructive force and the "undesirable" effects of decay as a creative tool, she bent the concrete forms until they cracked. For a short moment the fragments were held together only by wool, normally deemed the weaker material of the two. Then she reconfigured the slabs into arching three-dimensional forms and stabilised these tables with concrete.

STUDIO LIBERTINY
Tomáš Gabzdil Libertiny
1 The Paper Vase (Type 1)
2 The Paper Vase (Type 4)
3 The Paper Vase (Type 5)

"What is Nature?" was a question that we have found very interesting to play with and to think about. We didn't want to arrive at a specific answer but rather use the dialectic nature of it. We found the juxtaposition of two artifacts to be the most outspoken: the wood and the paper. Gluing 700 indentical prints, by hand, one by one, using wood glue and press resulted in solid block that had similar characteristcs as wood. We combined traditional woodworking techniques with meticulous repetitive labor and created The Paper Vases. The magic is that every page contains one single identical print that later appears distorted on the surface of the individual vases.

| 1 | 2 | 3 |

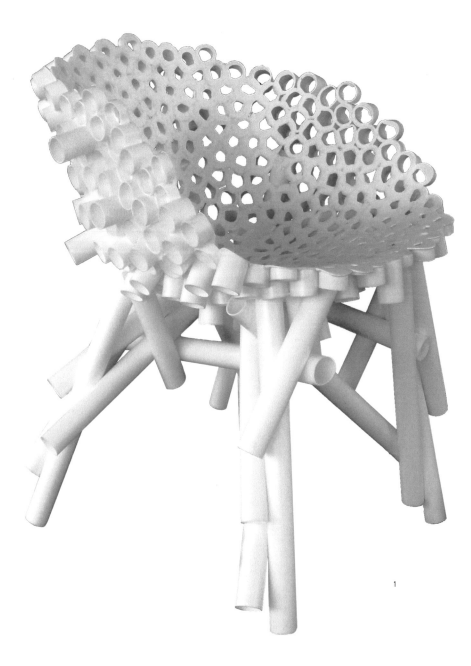

1 PP Tube #2 chair
This second version of the chair tests the strength of the material and process by reducing the amount of tube used, the number of legs and the number of welded joints.

2 PP Tube chair
For his first version of the PP Tube chair, Price heated and pressed a seat-shaped former into a stack of common plumbing tubes, the ends of which melted and fused together, leaving a pattern of irregular holes on the surface of the moulded seat.

3 PVC Hose chair
Price heated and pressed a seat-shaped former into a ball of clear PVC hose, which began to melt and, after prolonged exposure to the heat, to burn. Once cooled, the surface of the seat looked charred and brittle but was actually stable, resilient and comfortable.

4 PP Blue Rope chair
Price heated and pressed a seat-shaped former into a ball of polypropylene rope, which began to liquify. As it cooled, however, it set in the shape of a seat, creating a contrast in form and texture to the remaining rope.

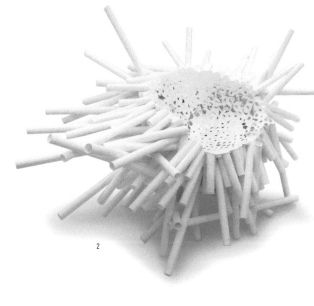

MAX LAMB
Poly chair

A process of destruction was used to create. Lamb carved a unique chair by hand from a block of expanded polystyrene and then coated in a fast-drying poyurethane rubber spray.

Starch chair

To create this water-soluble and bio-degradable foamed starch chair that can be left in the garden to compost after a summer's use, Lamb recycled 100% un-modified, foamed, dried and extruded starch (which had been factory waste) to create a very light and impact-resistant packaging loosefill. At the factory from which he salvaged his material, Lamb pressed the starch cylinders into the form of a seat with his hands (possible due to their moisture content) and then sat in it to form the seat and back – and a unique piece of furniture.

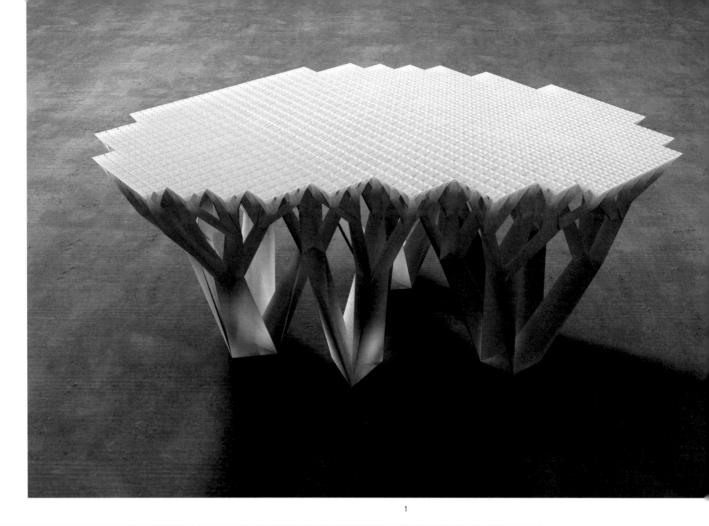

1

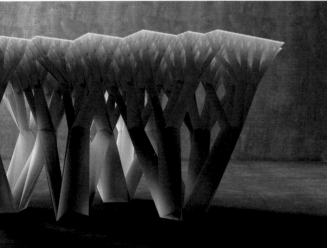

2

**PLATFORM STUDIO
WITH MATTHIAS BÄR**
Jan Wertel, Gernot Oberfell &
Matthias Bär

1,2 Fractal-T table
Both fragile and powerfully mineral-
looking, this luminous low table was
rapid-prototyped by Materialise.MGX.

AMANDA LEVETE

3 Especially For You.MGX bowl
A rapid-prototyped chromed bowl for
Materialise.MGX that looks like a pile
of scrap.

R&SIE
François Roche
I've Heard About (opposite)
A series of architectural models rapid-pro-
totyped by Materialise.MGX that depicts an
emerging and uncertain urban structure.

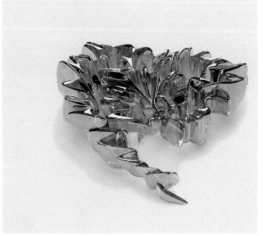

3

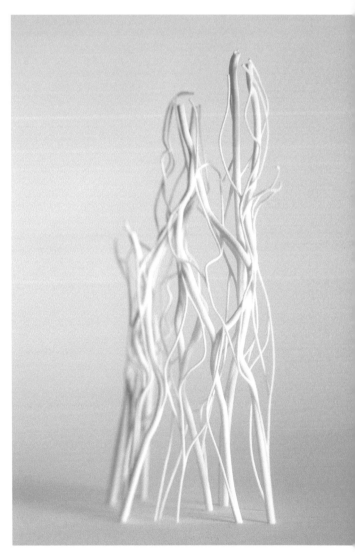

NENDO
Oki Sato
Pages 136–139

Japanese design office Nendo has earned so much critical praise that it's easy to think there are at least a couple of people behind it. Not so. Nendo is 30-year-old Canadian Oki Sato. Born in Canada but trained and now working in Tokyo, Sato studied architecture, established the studio in 2002 and branched out to Milan three years later. Sato's skills run the gamut from graphics and product, event and interior design to residential architecture. But it is the graceful inventiveness of his furniture that has won him accolades.

In 2006, Sato launched One Percent Products as its creative director, selecting furniture and tabletop pieces by various designers and producing only 100 of each in order "to give owners the chance to experience the joy of owning one percent." These pieces are sold online and include Sato's Hanabi pendant lamp, which, because it is made from shape-memory alloy, "blooms," its metal petals lifting upward to open the fixture when the light is turned on, and closing again when the light is extinguished and its heat fades. Also for One Percent, his Polar nesting tables change surface pattern: pulled apart, they look transparent but when layered, the polarising film on each surface produces various flower patterns depending on the degree of overlap.

In 2008, Nendo's pleated paper Cabbage chair was produced for the exhibition "XXlst Century Man" directed by fashion designer Issey Miyake at Tokyo's 21 21 Design Sight. Sato made Cabbage out of the masses of pleated wastepaper generated in the process of making Miyake's pleated fabric. He belted a roll of the paper and created a seat by peeling away its outer layers, one at a time. There was no need to finish the material or to use glues, nails or screws so, as Sato is well aware, the design is timely. It could allow the chair to be shipped in a compact roll (the end-user peels it), eliminating fabrication and lowering distribution costs while alleviating environmental concerns. It is this combination of pragmatic problem-solving and poetic form that has allowed Sato, and Nendo, to fire imaginations so rapidly.

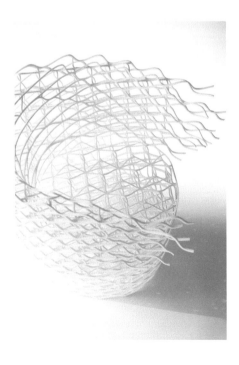

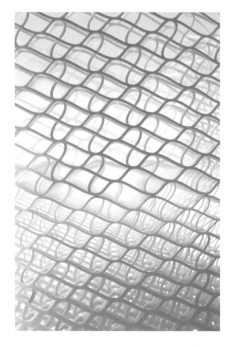

Diamond chair
The dense atomic structure of a diamond efficiently disperses strength and light throughout the material, giving diamonds their singular hardness and shine. Sato used this atomic array as a motif in devising a chair that would respond to pressure by absorbing rather than resisting it. His studio created this structure through a powder-sintered rapid prototyping technique that uses a laser to transform polyamide particles into a hard mould based on 3D CAD data. This method allowed the designers to add thickness where users need support, and to carve away the material in other areas to create greater resilience and comfort. In this way, one material served multiple purposes.

NENDO
Cabbage stool
Sato designed this chair using the pleated paper that is a byproduct, in massive amounts, of the process of making Issey Miyake's pleated fabric. By peeling down layers from a roll of pleated paper, one layer at a time, the consumer can create his own seat. Resins added during the original paper production process add strength and allow the material to retain its form, while the pleats themselves give the chair resilience. Since the production process is so simple, the chair could potentially be shipped in a compact roll and peeled at home.

THE TALETELLERS

HUMAN SCALE / COMIC STYLE / INNER SPACE / LOCAL / SIMPLE LIFE / CLUMSY AND SHY / HOME MADE / SLOW / URBAN RUSTIQUE

5.5 DESIGNERS / A4ADESIGN / BAS VAN DER VEER / BCXSY / BLESS / DITTE HAMMERSTRØM / DOSHI LEVIEN / DRIFT / FERNANDO & HUMBERTO CAMPANA / FRANK WILLEMS / FRÉDÉRIC RUYANT / GAM PLUS FRATESI / HALDANE MARTIN / HELLA JONGERIUS / HERME CISCAR & MÓNICA GARCÍA / HIROOMI TAHARA / INEKE HANS / JOEL DEGEMARK / KAREN RYAN / KATARINA HÄLL / KATRIN SONNLEITNER / KIKI VAN EIJK / KWANGHO LEE / LEIF.DESIGN-PARK / MAARTEN BAAS / MARTINO GAMPER / OD-V / OVERTREDERS W / PETER MARIGOLD / LOOL82 / RIJADA / STUDIO EDWARD VAN VLIET / STUDIO GORM / STUDIO MAKKINK & BEY / TARO & SARAH / TORD BOONTJE / WIS DESIGN / WOKMEDIA

THE TALETELLERS ARE ABLE TO EXPLOIT EVERYTHING THAT INDUSTRIAL SOCIETY HAS PRODUCED, THEY COLLECT THE RUBBISH GENERATED BY THAT SOCIETY AND TRANSFORM IT. THEY GIVE IT A HISTORY AND A CONTEXT THAT THEY WOULD VERY MUCH LIKE TO DENY.

The Taletellers among designers are addressing a major theme: in our post-industrial world, a world that has had all its magic removed, they long to poeticise the profane. They want to give some mystique back to the objects and rituals that accompany our everyday lives; they want to restore the significance they lost in the course of Modernism. Ultimately they abhor the industry as unworthy of humanity, but they know how to use it well. They are able to exploit everything that industrial society has produced, they collect the rubbish generated by that society and transform it. They infect it with emotions and associations from different epochs. They give it a history and a context that they would very much like to deny. They tell us tales, often too good to be true, sometimes cruel, but often with a moral to them.

Taletellers are a Postmodern phenomenon. This movement's first designs appeared in the early 90s, in Belgium and Holland, in the form of Martin Margiela's pullovers, which were sewn together from adapted army socks, or Tejo Remy's Chest of Drawers (1991), individual drawers made from people's bulky rubbish, held together by a belt to produce an object that was at least something like a chest of drawers. Who would have dreamt at the time that this kind of design using industrial society's leftovers would at some point become so influential all over the world? But the number of Taletellers has increased in recent decades, and the movement that started in the Benelux countries has turned into an international phenomenon. Taletellers can now come from Brazil or Korea, India or Japan. The fact is that material from a rotting affluent society is accumulating everywhere and it has to be transformed into something new.

Contrasts, breaks with what we have long been used to, imperfect things, these are the hallmarks of HELLA JONGERIUS designs. This Dutch designer made her name in the 1990s as a member of the Dutch "Droog Design" group. Jongerius's designs – such as flexible washbasins or rubber vases – were quick to attract international attention. She left "Droog Design" in 2000 and set up her own studio in Rotterdam. Its name, "Jongeriuslab", suggests what her work is all about: experiments. Ceramics, wood, rubber and glass appear in

strange combinations here. But her forms also address set-pieces from our collective memory. So her Polder sofa for the furniture-object manufacturer Vitra represents something like a move in another direction. It was part of the company's new Home Collection, started in 2005. And the Polder sofa is indeed reminiscent of a polder, or of pontoons that have been fastened together, floating aimlessly somewhere off the Dutch coast – asymmetrically arranged cuboids and cushions in the same shape, in brown and beige covers. A year later, Jongerius presented her armchair called The Worker for Vitra, a chair that looks like a Victorian wing chair because of its low seat and high back, but that seems to have fallen into the hands of the American Shaker sect because of its material quality and formal lankiness. Jongerius combines wood with aluminium, and leather with textiles for the cushions and covers. She connects craft and high-tech. And the result is something that could rightly be called digital craft. In 2008 she developed the Rotterdam Chair for Vitra, her first stacking chair, which looks like a wooden garden chair, but has some details that confirm it as a genuine Jongerius. One of these features is a coloured plastic gusset at the back of the seat that gives the entire object a somewhat questionable and imperfect air – which is exactly how Hella Jongerius sees the world. Another feature is that the chair legs are decorated with stoppers in the same material. And last but not least, we must mention her Office Pets for the 2007 Vitra Edition. These are three fabulous creatures, made in a limited edition, whose role seems to be to lend a hint of magic to the modern office. Animal-like textile bodies grow out of typical office chair feet, friendly companions who probably won't do your work for you, but who will at least be able to lift your spirits.

Hella Jongerius/Blossom

And it is precisely lifting their clients' spirits that seems to motivate other Taletellers from Jongerius's homeland. Take Joris Laarman from Utrecht, for example. He drew attention to himself in 2003 with his re-inventing functionality project, in which he gave a radiator a rococo look and was also in a position to argue convincingly for its effectiveness as a heating device thanks to the large surface area available for transmitting warmth. At the time of writing, Laarman is working on the detail of his Bone Chair project, a chair whose statics try to imitate the human skeleton. Absorbing force exerted from the outside and using a skeleton

Ineke Hans/Country Rock

structure as a means for doing this is a subject pursued in automobile research, and this is where Laarman found allies to help him with his idea. Even if the necessity of a shock absorber like those used in car travel does not suggest itself immediately for sitting still on a chair, Laarman's results are still definitely worth looking at. In fact his Bone Chair looks like the discovery of a primeval species in the sitting culture world that was hitherto unknown to us.

The Dutch designer INEKE HANS is also a Taleteller, armed with a Master's in Furniture Design from the Royal College of Art in London. Her furniture and accessories seem to be not of

Kiki van Eijk/Quilt chair

this world. They are literally fabulous; a comic landscape of a very appealing kind. Everything seems somehow childlike in its proportions – big heads with big eyes, set on squat bodies and making viewers feel sympathy above all. Then we have the KIKI & JOOST practise, set up by Kiki van Eijk and Joost van Bleiswijk, two graduates of the Eindhoven Design Academy who

have established themselves in the field of reviving historic furniture types – screens, rocking chairs, bureaux and showcases – and shifting them into the present day with complete respect for the Baroque or Biedermeier forms and decoration. And finally there is TORD BOONTJE. After studying design in Eindhoven and London, in 1996 he set up his own design practice with his wife, the British glass artist Emma Woffenden. Boontje made his name with the "Transglass" vase series, created in 1997, and with his 1998 Rough and Ready furniture – held together with adhesive tape and lashing straps and made from timber offcuts with

Tord Boontje/Witches' Kitchen

blankets as upholstery. Today Boontje is one thing above all others – a florist. His flowery designs for Kvadrat, Moroso or Habitat are omnipresent; he covers the world with seas of flowers, some lasered from metal, some printed on fabric. Boontje has helped design to vegetate.

Martino Gamper/Sonet Butterfly

But there are Taletellers at work in other places too. MARTINO GAMPER of Merano has found his way to London. He took on an extraordinary bet: that he would design one hundred different chairs in one hundred days, and of course he would build them himself. He did not embark on this major project without some start-up material; in fact he dismantled existing chairs, mainly found standard furniture, and rapidly reassembled the material to make new chairs. Gamper simply rewrote a hundred stories in this way. The DOSHI LEVIEN practice is also based in London, run by Jonathan Levien and Nipa Doshi. Their work

links different cultures. Nipa Doshi is strongly influenced her Indian origins and culture, Levien's thinking bears a Western stamp and is guided by industrial processes. The two of them designed the My Beautiful Backside seating collection for Moroso in 2008. The designers tell us that the

Doshi Levien/My Beautiful Backside

idea for this enchanting ensemble, which is in fact driven by a formal language that is new, luxuriant and rich in detail for Western eyes, came from a miniature painting showing a maharani on the floor of her palace, surrounding by a large number of different kinds of cushions an upholstery.

The brothers FERNANDO AND HUMBERTO CAMPANA from São Paolo can probably be called South America's most important designers at the present time. To create their unmistakable style – often summed up as "tropical modern – the Campanas combine everyday objects, usually taken from the lives of poor people in the favelas, to make playful furniture designs that all seem to be full of stories. The materials they use for their designs include plastic hoses or film, untreated timber, cables, car tyres or cuddly toys. There is scarcely a product of our throwaway society that the Campanas have not been

able to take as a reusable raw material and transform it into one of their wondrous ready-mades. Take the Terrastool for the Kreo gallery (2007), a conical clay solid containing an upright roll of fabric as a seat, or the Transplastic series of lamps – a floating light sculpture created from artfully draped plastic film that seems to carry the

F. & H. Campana/TransRock Chair

circular lights as a support material. We also have the TransNeomatic project, a series of trays and etageres that was manufactured in Vietnam from used rubber tyres and a rattan core. For the Campanas, work always means seeking out an independent Brazilian identity, an identity that does not bear the stamp of European immigrants, but is rooted in the fusion of cultures within their homeland. The Campanas are trying to give this fusion culture a voice with their work.

Increasing numbers of Taletellers are now appearing in the Far East as well. LEIF.DESIGNPARK, for example, founded by the Japanese designers Takashi Ueno, Mamoru Naito and Keizaburo Honda. They deliberately choose to work on artistic projects, as well as interior and industrial design. Their furni-

ture – whether intended for children or adults – has a playful quality and kindly essential traits, as though inspired by good spirits. The practise takes the name design park seriously and literally. All their objects show a kind of cultivated naturalness. No entrance barriers need to be passed

Leif.Designpark/Kukunochi

to be able to involve ourselves in them, just as in a public park. The Korean designer KWANGHO LEE wove metre-long wires into hoses like bowls and brushes in his Weave Your Lightning project, and these are then used as supports for various lamps. Kwangho Lee explains these mystical looking installations in terms of his own childhood experiences. He says that the image of his mother knitting pullovers is so strongly associated with his carefree childhood that he used it as the starting point for his ideas when creating objects. Mother and childhood as design models?

Taletellers inevitably have to put up with being criticised for producing mainly sentimental kitsch. They cannot really object to this, as they know that the need for kitsch of this kind will grow as society becomes more modern and content. Kitsch flourishes best in a germ-free environment. It is only there that feelings can be released again and discharge themselves in the refuse of our modern civilization – like a memory of days long gone that we carry with us as a programme that cannot be deleted.

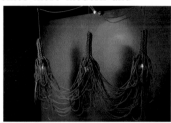

Kwangho Lee/Weave your lighting-Last of three

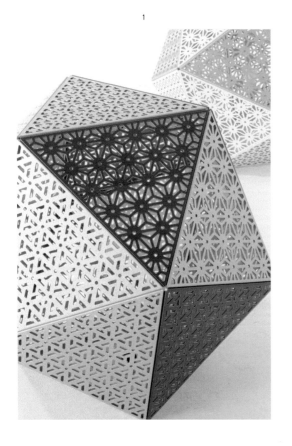

STUDIO EDWARD VAN VLIET
Edward van Vliet
1 Rontonton lantern
2 Donut pouf
3 Juju chair
4 Sushi sofa

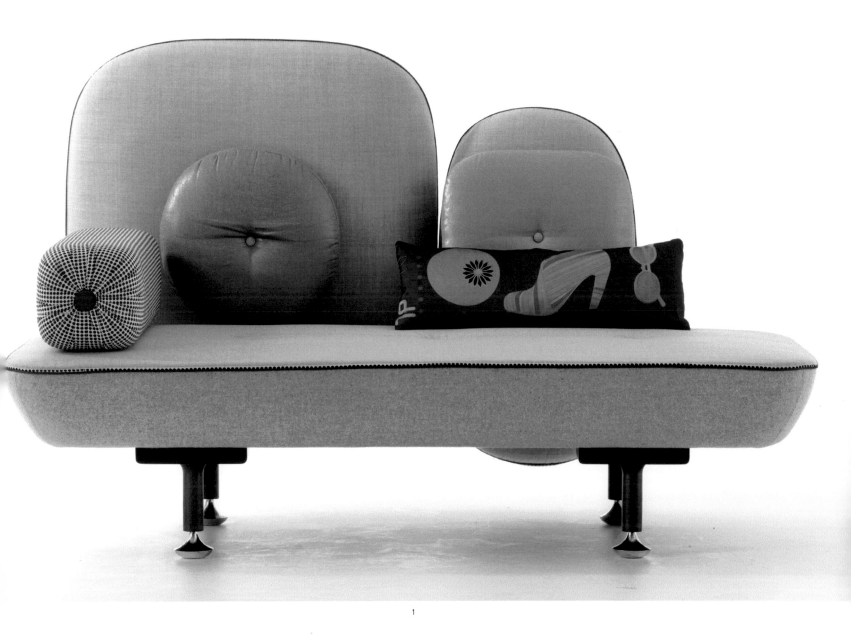

1

DOSHI LEVIEN

1,2 My Beautiful Backside sofa
As well-designed as its name, and
inspired by a miniature painting of an
Indian princess in her palace, sitting
amongst a pile of cushions, My Beautiful Backside features floating cushions
in unusual colours and shapes. Over-
size badges serving as buttons embel-
lish the seat as one might accessorize
an item of clothing.

3 Charpoy daybed
A range of daybeds that marry the
skilled workmanship of Indian seam-
sters with Italian industrial production.
Meaning four legs, Charpoy is based
on the ubiquitous Indian daybed. The
Charpoys are entirely hand-embroi-
dered with details including the ancient national dice game of "chaupar".
The game resembles chess and led to
the war of "Mahabharata", at a time
when kingdoms and wives were waged
as prizes.

4 Principessa daybed
A daybed consisting of many thin
mattresses, the topmost displaying a
graphic array of objects belonging to
a contemporary princess preparing for
a night on the town.

2

3

4

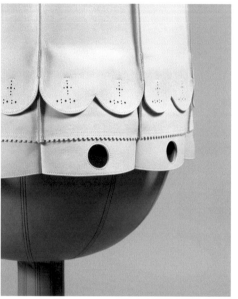

1

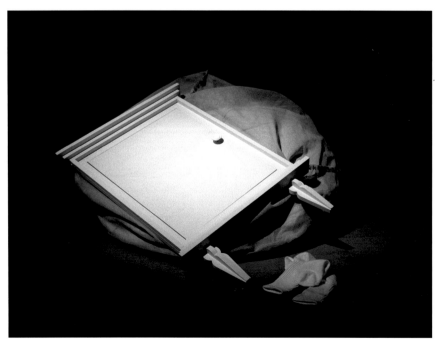

2

JONGERIUSLAB
Hella Jongerius
1 Office Pets objects

KATRIN SONNLEITNER
2 Möbelette chest of drawers
Setting the disorderly pile (nature) against the orderly stack (culture), this chest of drawers chooses chaos over convention. Messes disappear into the sack until needed next but without the rigidity of an ordinary dresser. And as is typical, changes take place inside: what is put in clean and folded comes out rumpled in the end.

1

DITTE HAMMERSTRØM

1 Wrinkle sofa

2 Bistro light
   An upholstered chair with slightly
   distorted proportions, which enable
   new ways of using it. The chairs are
   industrially made, but due to the nature
   of the upholstery process, each chair
   becomes unique.

2

DITTE HAMMERSTRØM
Socialising sofas
A group of sofas that gather together to
form a environment for socialising. The
sofa creates a room within a room that is
best-suited to gatherings and parties.

DITTE HAMMERSTRØM

Loungescape sofa

A sofa in seven pieces that can be configured in various ways according to the layout of the room and the anticipated use and then bound together.

149

KIK!
Kiki van Eijk
1 Quilt chair
2 Quilt stool
A rocking chair and stool with cubistic construction elements of steel and upholstery that are made using traditional quilting techniques to make them look padded and buttoned, and giving them a soft feel.

FRANK WILLEMS
3 Hello Dolly bench
A stool that is both cuddly and firm.

FRANK WILLEMS

1 Plus de Madam Rubens seating
Madam Rubens is a mature and chubby lady who has just had an extreme makeover. Researching how to extend the life of various types of waste, Willems found that mattresses are rarely repurposed. By folding and adding finish to discarded mattresses, he created bulky, comfortable seats. Folding the mattresses differently and using various legs, he created a unique lady every time.

2 Petit Pouf
Pouf made from discarded mattresses.

3,4 Madam Rubens seating
Seating made from discarded mattresses.

151

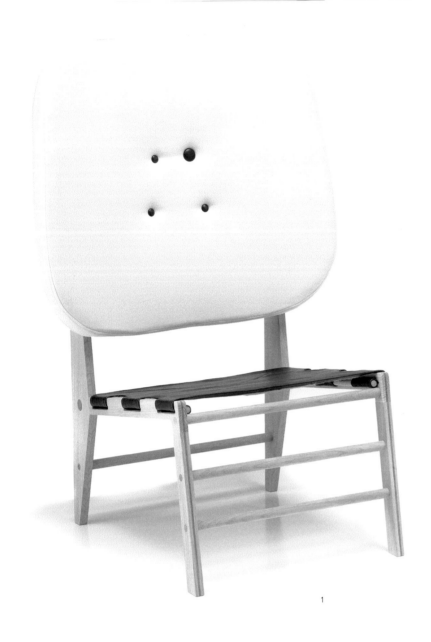

1

2

3

4

5

INEKE HANS

1 Country Rock rocking chair
Sober wooden furniture that apparently goes back to basics. At second glance, however, the texture in the wood isn't quite right: artificial and natural woodgrain are used together.

2 Fracture furniture
Lightweight polystyrene pieces that eschew structure but which are wrapped as if in a medical cast with a surprising new polyester plaster material that makes them extremely strong within a few minutes. The polyester bonding gives the group the appearance of being covered in a textile.

3 Country Sit and Country Side chairs
Sober wooden furniture that apparently goes back to basics. At second glance, however, the texture in the wood isn't quite right: artificial and natural woodgrain are used together.

1

2

3

1

DITTE HAMMERSTRØM
1 Sofa Set
Hammerstrøm seems to relate to
designed objects as if they were people. "Furniture tends to assemble in
groups," she insists. "Here, it has gone
one step further." By colliding entirely.

KATARINA HÄLL
2 Save furniture
The pieces take their cues from what
is left behind and forgotten inside the
barred windows and padlocked doors
of derelict and abandoned houses.

2

1

2

BCXSY
Boaz Cohen & Sayaka Yamamoto
1 Noisy Furniture LE
A modular furniture system in which
each element attaches to the next via
a Dual Lock re-closable fastener. This
allows various constructions ranging
from modest to wild.

WIS DESIGN
2 Decades chest of drawers
Drawers salvaged from flea markets and
collaged together regardless of style
and then unified by a white lacquered
MDF frame.

FRÉDÉRIC RUYANT
3 Mobilier National workspace

3

1

2

BLESS
3 File hammock
4 Sofa hammock
   A series of absurdly pragmatic hammock designs created to provide what Bless call "climate confusion assistance."

5 Art Cologne installation
   An installation including Bless's Fur Hammock (50% cotton, 50% coyote fur), mobile and "wallscape" (wallcovering)

6 Wallscape #9a Walter Piano
   An interior with printed wallcovering.

3

5

6

4

BLESS
Fat Knit hammock
Part of a series of absurdly pragmatic
hammock designs created to provide what
Bless call "climate confusion assistance."

KWANGHO LEE

1 ZIP stool
Celebrating nostalgia, Lee used the familiar remains of harvest season, large bundles of rice straw, by belting them and cutting off their scragly tops to create seating. He called it "zip" because this is the word in Korean for rice straws and because it also sounds like the English word "zip" as in "zipped" (compressed) – which they are.

LOOL82

Naty Moskovich

2 Box Life furniture
To bring quotidian Israel into the rarified gallery space and into the design industry, and to demonstrate the great design that happens daily without the help of designers, Moskovich grafted crates onto random elements of recycled furniture.

FRANK WILLEMS

3 Goldilocks Collection
A furniture series inspired by the personal preference shown and choices made in the tale of Goldilocks and the Three Bears. The three chairs don't have a fixed seat, so the user must create the seat they like by playing with a pile of cushions. The number, the colour or the softness of the cushions is undetermined. The table looks massive, but using different leg-sizes can modify its height.

STUDIO MAKKINK & BEY
Rianne Makkink & Jurgen Bey

1 Cleaning-Beauty-Dining-Table
Studio Makkink & Bey's Cleaning-Beauty-Dining-Table is filled with hand-painted porcelain plates and bowls, bone china cutlery, embroidered napkins and table mats, as well as other surprises.

2 Cleaning-Beauty-Locker
Jurgen Bey and architect Rianne Makkink's Studio Makkink & Bey have reinvented traditional Chinese art and craft techniques with their highly conceptual "Cleanliness is next to godliness" series, commissioned by Contrasts Gallery. Inspired by the beauty and optimism of Chinese propaganda posters, the pair reimagined propaganda for household cleaning by using precious Chinese porcelain, silk fabrics, woodwork, and reverse inside painting to re-create the humblest objects in the home. Cleaning cabinets are made luxurious and filled with gloves and aprons embroidered with cleaning ladies, a delicate porcelain mop, broom, dustpan and other reinvented objects.

OVERTREDERS W
Reinder Bakker/Hester van Dijk

3 Karavaan meeting point
Karavaan is a traveling theatre festival for which Overtreders W designed the meeting point, consisting of a transport container, 400 identical stools and a dance floor. The stools are strapped together to make various furniture, including a bar, tables and chairs. While moving to the next location, the stools are packed into the container, which can be used as a ticket booth once the festival is re-installed.

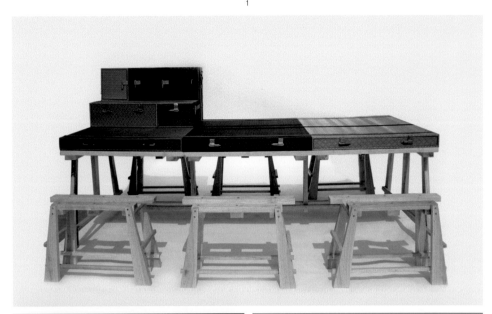

1

2

3

1

2

3

OD-V
Onno Donkers
Pages 152, 160, 166

As a handwritten note is to an email, so is OD-V furniture and interiors to other modern confections: expressive instead of boilerplate, specific instead of generalised, candid instead of rehearsed. The OD-V design studio and workshop based in Schiedam, the Netherlands is run by 1999 Design Academy Eindhoven graduate, Onno Donkers. Donkers' furniture and interiors eschew sleek polish and are, instead, highly contextual assemblages often using existing products and architectural elements as their raw materials. It is an aesthetic that is as effective as it is rough, endowing space with strong character and removing it from the realm of the generic.

For Nuits Blanches, a temporary hotel set up during Rotterdam's 2006 international film festival, Donkers constructed "shower tents" with funnel-shaped curtains that made for roomy bathing. The same year, he designed the interiors of Proef restaurants in both Rotterdam and Amsterdam, exposing old beams and surface blemishes but leaving the space bare.

In 2007, Donkers collaged together existing objects to create a furniture series and, in effect, an interior for Berlin's Bonanza Coffee Heroes shop. The shop featured seating, tables and food display surfaces created by perching MDF board atop stacks of coloured plastic crates. His "pallet-bar" was a bolted together collection of wood, pipes, and aluminum sheeting. This generated surfaces at various heights that then served various purposes, as well as allowing a piece of furniture that was actually bulky to preserve sightlines through the room. Donkers also assembled wall-anchored café tables from aluminum and existing desktops. The improvised look gives the space a strong point of view, combining cosiness with sophistication. In this Donkers is very Dutch: he can design space that is very opinionated without alienating anyone.

---

1 Pallet Bar
2 Legs chairs
3 Branch table
4 Crate–Top furniture
   By placing a crate-top on top of
   a crate, Donkers created a normal
   chair. By adding more crates he
   made a table-top, bar counter and
   other furniture elements.

5 Aluminium table

4

5

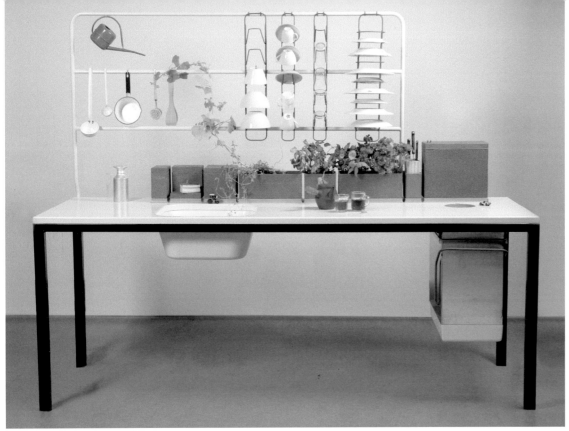

STUDIO GORM
John Arndt
Flow and the Kitchen of Terrestrial Mechanics

Mating nature and technology, Arndt sought to develop a new kind of kitchen environment where appliances and processes become part of an organic, intuitive system, efficiently utilising energy, waste, water and other natural resources. Flow is a system in which materials "flow" through multiple applications instead of being only partially used and then disposed of, where food is grown, stored, cooked and composted to grow more food. For this new space several products were developed that utilise and illustrate different natural processes and which can be used independently but are far more effective when used in concert within the larger system. The water from the dish rack drips on the herbs and edible plants which are grown in the planter boxes places below the rack. The countertop features a built-in waste bowl that can be used to dump scraps while preparing food. Once the bowl is full, it need only be tipped over to transfer the waste into the worm bin composter, located beneath the counter. As the waste is lowered into the composter, the worms convert it into nutrient rich fertilizer, which can then be returned to the plants.

TORD BOONTJE
Witches' Kitchen

1 The artisans of Brazil's Coopa-Rocca women's cooperative (who also made Artecnica's Design with Conscience Come Rain Come Shine lamp) create the all-black, hand-sewn line of Kitchen couture. They tailor a fringed Witches' Apron and Witches' Glove potholder for women, and a patchwork Wizards' Apron and Wizards' Glove potholder for men.

2 Guatemalan artisans hand-carve an intricate assortment of wooden utensils out of locally sourced sustainable and reforested wood. These utensils evoke a witch's essential tools, including a dagger knife and a pair of salad tossers shaped like witch's hands, in addition to a variety of double-ended serving forks and spoons.

3,4 Witches' Kitchen cookware is hand-moulded by Colombian artisans using a centuries-old pottery technique, and is embellished with textured leaf prints using a method developed by Artecnica and the artisans involved.

1

2

3

4

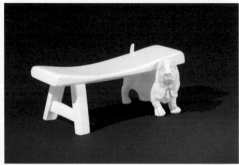

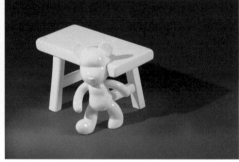

1

WOKMEDIA
Julie Mathias &
Wolfgang Kaeppner
1 Made in China furniture
Featuring traditional Chinese furniture
embedded with hand-carved wooden toys
and finished in white lacquer, the series
is a result of the designers' extended stay
in China as part of a collaboration with
Contrasts Gallery in Shanghai.

BAS VAN DER VEER
2 Multiculti planter/vase
The individual pots allow users to grow
a variety of herbs on their table while
representing diverse cultures, making
a lovely metaphorical and edible salad
when tossed together. Multiculti can
also be used as a cluster of vases.

2

1

2

1

2

FRÉDÉRIC RUYANT
1 Cabinet de Lecture seating
2 Confident Pour Soi seating

OD-V
Onno Donkers
3 Trojan Horse vista
This installation was part of a project for Gallery Saekkers. Users were invited to climb the installation and lie down with a friend to enjoy the view.

4 Shower Tents
The funnel-shaped shower curtains make these baths very comfortable.

3

4

This series uses a simple geometric principle: the inverted angles of a shape split into pieces will always add up to 360°. The angles can be interchanged but will always form a whole.

1

2

3

STUDIO MAKKINK & BEY
Rianne Makkink & Jurgen Bey
Pages 159, 168–171, 229, 268, 269

Jurgen Bey and architect Rianne Makkink of Rotterdam-based Studio Makkink & Bey who weave whole narratives through their product, furniture and interior design. Bey has long been known for his investigations into everything from urban planning and dust to the ways that people wait, in order to create objects faithful to the way we (wish we could) live. And through these objects and environments the stories he tells about people come through with great wisdom and clarity. It is this curiosity about the reciprocal relationship between people and objects that drives the innovation and poetry of Makkink and Bey's work.

The Slow Car for Vitra, for instance, is a rethinking of urban personal and work space. While a slower (40 km/h speed limit) vehicle would positively affect road safety and the environment, it could also remake interstitial spaces into space suited to work and socialising. Personsised mobile interiors would give city dwellers a reason to slow down, or even stop, to smell the roses.

In early 2008, Makkink & Bey transformed a stack of wooden 2x4s and a long bolt of wool felt into a temporary home at La Galerie de Pierre Bergé & Associés. The Witness Flat was constructed by patching together felt swatches and wood slats, to create improvised furniture like a stuffed straight-back chair, a desk with integrated chandelier, a pair of armchairs that were pixelated images of themselves, and a traditional spindle-back chair wrapped in a bulky knitted "sweater" that exposed bits of two legs and one arm. The studio also made microarchitecture in early 2008 for Pearl Lam's Contrasts Gallery in China. For Contrasts, the pair sewed together a vibrantly colorful, modern version of the traditional Chinese home, featuring bed, bath and simple rectilinear storage pieces. Furniture elements included the Cleaning-Beauty-Bathtub, a handcrafted porcelain tub with a sculpted lid to keep the water warm. The canopied bed was hung with intricately cut paper curtains while the wardrobe resembled a jewelbox. Drawers wrapped in jewel-toned silk fabrics opened to reveal delicate cotton garments and white gloves with embroidered fingers. In nearly contradictory material, colour and cultural palettes, Makkink & Bey have recounted twin scenes of lush domesticity and sensual ornamentation. If only we could bring it home.

Witness Flat domestic interior
1 Wardrobe
2 Pair of nightstands
3 Extendable table
4 Desk with integrated chandelier
5 Pixelated chairs
6 Pixelated triptych
7 Pixelated sideboard
8 Pixelated side table
   Dutch trees (wood slats), sheep (felt strips) and a sewing machine were used to make an eclectic collection of furniture that transformed La Galerie de Pierre Bergé & Associés into a temporary house.

1

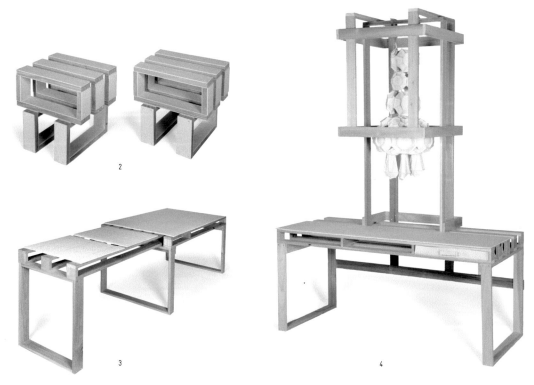

2

3

4

5

6

7

8

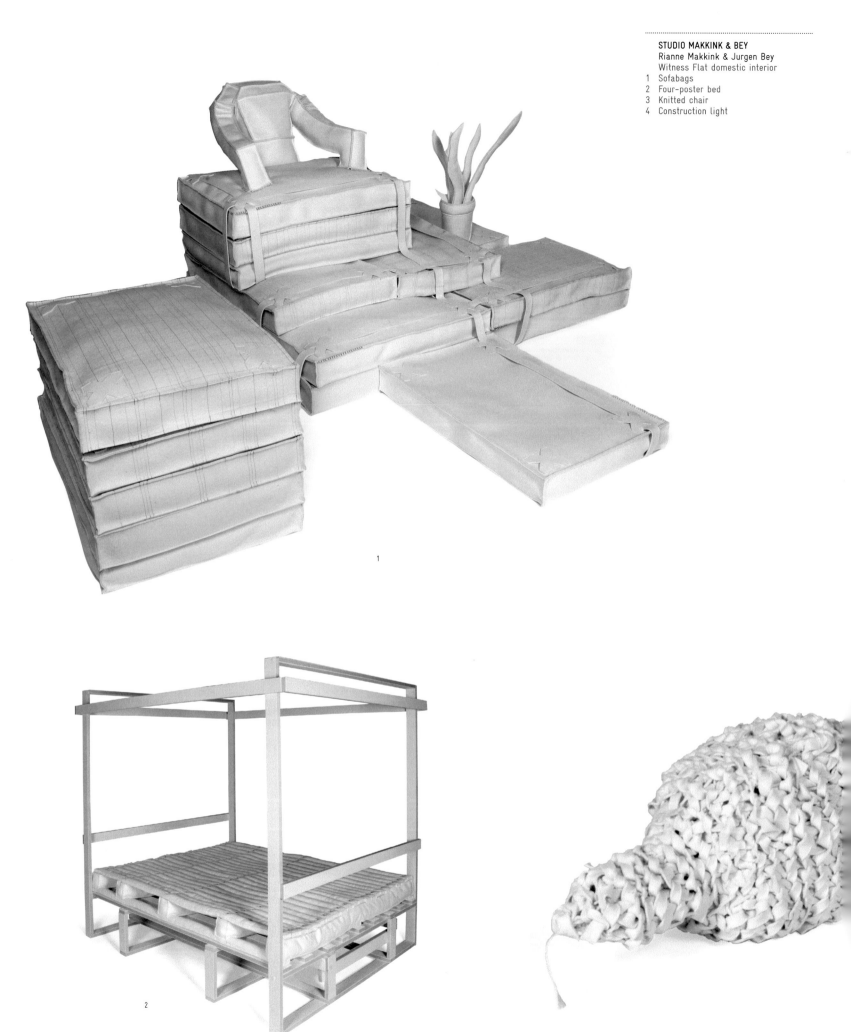

STUDIO MAKKINK & BEY
Rianne Makkink & Jurgen Bey
Witness Flat domestic interior
1 Sofabags
2 Four-poster bed
3 Knitted chair
4 Construction light

3

4

FEHLING & PEIZ
Yvonne Fehling, Jennie Peiz
Page 172

People don't only need epic novels, we also need little poems, suggest Karlsruhe-based Yvonne Fehling and Jennie Peiz whose Kleine Gärten chair's green sod seat is intended to supplement the city's gardens and parks with a patch of personal grass, a verdant little poem.

Fehling & Peiz's interventions are poetic, however, as often as they are practical. Usually they are both. The studio's Re* series mends used and damaged objects (chairs, dishware) and in the process renders them not just re-usable but precious. Shady Shade pendant lamps, produced under their brand name Kraud, are made from CNC-cut paper glued together and resemble hives of beeswax with asymmetrical, ragged sections that make them look like an act of nature. The Wick Elleuchte is a bulb wrapped with its own electrical cord, the way a ball of yarn is wound, so that it becomes both a potential extension cord and a lampshade. Stitch Graffiti mimics the creep of ivy over a building's façade – using thick yarn. (While studying at the Hogeschule für Gestaltung in Karlsruhe, Fehling used the façade as canvas for the first time, mounting a Toilette sign to a local wall with an arrow indicating a corner bleached by a history of repeated urination.)

For the Richard Meier-designed Arp Museum that opened in Germany in the fall of 2007, Fehling & Peiz contributed a dozen wooden benches called Stuhlhockerbank. Stuhlhockerbank is a small series of oil-finished oak seats that generate public social space by seamlessly joining multiple traditional carved straightback chairs (or, depending on how you see it, by adding clusters of traditional backrests to an unusually meandering bench) to create a playful multiperson seating element. Chair, stool, bench – it is all three. Traditional, modern? Both simultaneously. Sculpture or design? Both again. A little longer piece of poetry.

Stuhlhockerbank public seating
A series of seating for public spaces that acts simultaneously as chair, stool and bench. Beyond their seating function, however, the objects also have narrative elements. They seem familiar and yet, at the same time, surprising.

1

3

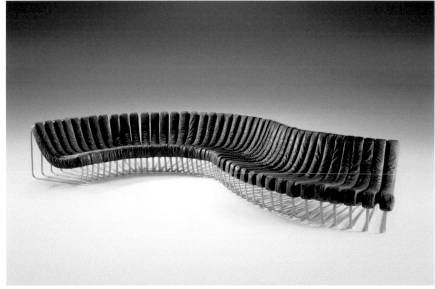

2

KAREN RYAN
Custom-Made seating
A series of one-off seats made
with second-hand chairs, paint
adn plastic ties.

MARTINO GAMPER
100 Chairs in 100 Days
1 Ghost
2 Two-Some
3 Bare Light
4 Phiippe Fantastique
5 Barbapapa in Vienna
6 Cathedra Rassa
7 Multiple Choice
8 Painters Mate
Using discarded and donated chairs, Gamper cobbled together 100 new chairs from pieces of existing ones in 100 days.

1
2

3
4

5
6

7
8

1

design
the
wonderland

2

3

4

A4ADESIGN

1 For Kids Only playhouse
An architecture dedicated to play, made
from recycled honeycomb cardboard.

2 Wonderland bench/bookcase

3 Macro objects
Objects made from recycled honey
comb cardboard to define rest areas at
the 2005 Pitti Uomo Expositions.

4 Fuordacqua objects
Fluttering objects inspired by flowers
and sea life, a joint-fit assembly made
from recycled honeycombed cardboard.

LEIF.DESIGNPARK

1 Tou chair
Tou combines warm woven materials and traditional Japanese craft with a modern form. The rattan backrest and seat are intricately hand-woven through an upholstered frame.

2 Lin bench
3 Lin chair
A solid wood leg frame raises the upholstered forms of the Lin pieces, enhancing their appearance of floating.

1

2

3

FERNANDO AND HUMBERTO CAMPANA
TransRock chair (TransPlastic Collection)
The Campanas narrate a fictional story
suggesting that in today's world of synthetic materials, it becomes reasonable to
imagine the growth of hybrid, natural/ar-
tificial, objects. They envision the woven
Acui fibres in these pieces to be assimilat-
ing the plastic of the seating and lighting
in a way similar to an immunological response. Nature grows out of the man-made
and overpowers it.

1

RIJADA
Rihards Funts
1   Dogie multifunctional furniture
2   Synthetic Birdhouse light

3   Find Me playhouse
    Designed for children aged between two
    and six, this playhouse promotes self-
    expression and creativity. After use, the
    house can be recycled or, the designer
    suggests, framed like painting.

2   3

5.5 DESIGNERS

1 Collection BAC

2 Mon Beau Sapin floor lamp
A light made from a Parisian 2007
Christmas (fir) tree trunk in a limited
edition of 10 numbered pieces.

1

2

1

2

1

FRANK WILLEMS

1 Tape-it tape

A transparant tape with a fairytale printed on it. Like every fairytale, it combines
sweet elements, and frightening ones.
The longer one looks at the tape, the
stranger the tale becomes. Butterflies flut-
ter to flowers that grow out of an eyeball
with a monkey walking on top of it. Rein-
vent that boring lamp, the old cupboard, a
chair, vase or the whole room.

WOKMEDIA
Julie Mathias & Wolfgang Kaeppner,
in collaboration with Michael Cross

2 Lununganga shelf

This shelf is a response to the flooded,
jungle environment the designers were
thrown into when they went to work in
Sri Lanka after the 2006 tsunami. They
preserved the image of partially sub-
merged trees by translating it into shelves
that assume both the qualities of the
overgrown lake that surrounded us and
the tranquility of European furniture.

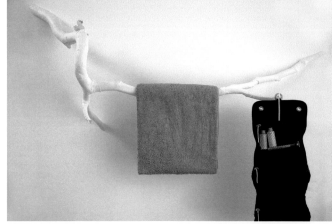

2

DRIFT
Lonneke Gordijn

1 Dandelights
This tiny piece of real nature uses batteries to grow, representing a fusion of nature and technology. The poetic light is made from phosphorus bronze, LED lights and real dandelion seeds. Each piece is numbered and arrives with a signed letter and instructions for how to care for the Dandelight.

2 Fragile Future lighting
A modular lighting system that seems to creep over the wall like a plant. Each module consists of a visible circuit connected to a dandelion light. Connect up to 50 modules easily, each in five different ways, making various compositions possible. The designers' second fusion of nature and technology, the installation can be programmed to "protect" itself by pretending to be out of order when a person comes too close, using sensors and a chip.

1

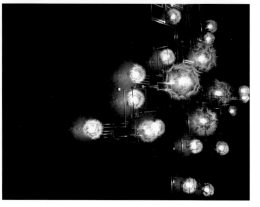

2

186

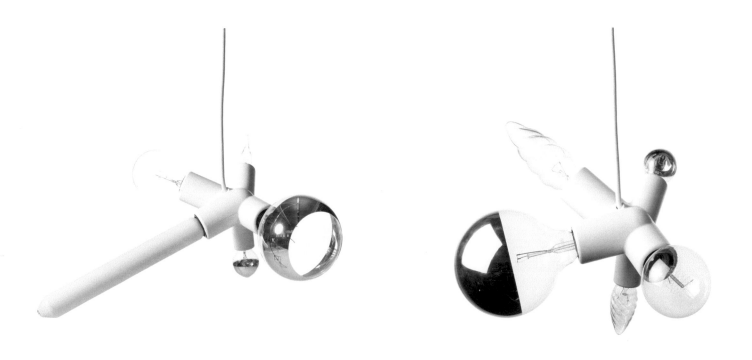

KWANGHO LEE
Weave Your Lighting Series
1 Last of Three
2 C+
3 Black Waterfall
4 White Brush
5 B Chain

Inspired by his mother's knitting during his childhood, Lee was reminded of the happy days of his youth by her knitted sweaters and mittens. Using electric wire as yarn, he began to knit his own pieces. Instead of knitting with needles, Lee weaves single long wires into draping webs that form the shades.

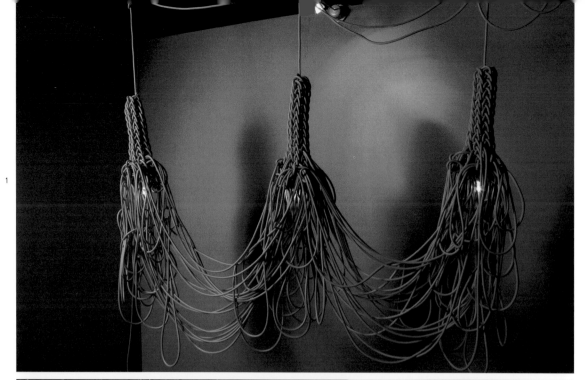

3

4

5

LEIF.DESIGNPARK

1 KuKunochi Lounge
The meaning of "KuKunochi" is the guardian that protects the forest and nature. This concept is grounded in Japanese traditional fantasy, and the branches growing from the large, impressive base imply this. The combination of the soft texture of the seat cover (urethane foam) and the symbolic forms of the back (made of white ash) is also a significant feature. The idea was inspired by an image of nature, combined with the calm that exists in a traditional Japanese garden.

2 Lin Pod bench prototype
and Cele floor lamp
3,4 Exhibition at the Milan furniture fair's satellite show (2008)
5 Ketta kid's chair

1

LEIF.DESIGNPARK

1 Exhibition at the Milan furniture fair's satellite show (2007)

2 Tone Series prototype
3 Tone chair
4 Tone dining table
5 Tone kid's table

The Tone project is an attempt to produce furniture using materials and skills long established in the Japanese culture. The design recalls traditional Japanese parquetry, interpreted in a modern way. Craftsmen have historically used parquetry to bring out the natural character of the various types of wood they use. The natural colours of the wood result from trees' absorption of nutrients in the soil. The Tone series uses a selection of sustainable timbers, flaunting the native colour and grain differences.

2

3

4

5

1

2

LEIF.DESIGNPARK
1 Tone kid's chair prototype
2,3 Tone Series prototypes
Leif.designpark wants children to be
brought up in close proximity to, and
touching, natural and environment-
friendly materials.

3

···

THE ENTERTAINERS

SUPER HYPER/PIMP STYLE/RANDOM HISTORY/ ARTISTIC ATTITUDE/TRANSFORMATION/ TRASH/BLOB/WASTED SPACE

···

ANNA IRINARCHOS/ANNA JAMES/ARIK BEN SIMHON/BANK & RAU/BARBER OSGERBY/BARLAS BAYLAR/ BAS UPON/BAS VAN DER VEER/BRAM BOO/COMMITTEE/CRISTIAN ZUZUNAGA/CULDESAC/DAN GRAHAM/DANIEL BECKER/DING3000/ERNESTO NETO/F. AKASAKA DESIGN/FORM US WITH LOVE/ FOR USE/FRANZ ACKERMANN/FRÉDÉRIC RUYANT/FRONT/GABRIELLE AMMANN ‖ DESIGNER'S GAL-LERY/HAYON STUDIO/HECTOR SERRANO/HOW ABOUT VIKTOR/JAIME HAYON/JANTZE BROGÅRD ASSHOFF/JOHANNA GRAWUNDER/JOOST VAN BLEISWIJK/KATRIN SONNLEITNER/KIKI VAN EIJK/ KJELLGREN KAMINSKY/KONSTANTIN GRCIC INDUSTRIAL DESIGN/LIFEGOODS/MALIN LUNDMARK/ MARCEL WANDERS/MARC NEWSON/MAARTEN BAAS/MASSIMO BARTOLINI/MATHIAS BENGTSSON/ MINALE-MAEDA/MIN CHEN/NIKA ZUPANC/OLAFUR ELIASSON/PEPE HEYKOOP/PER EMANUELSSON & BASTIAN BISCHOFF/PHIL CUTTANCE/PHILIP EDIS/PHILIPPE MALOUIN/PIEKE BERGMANS/POSTFOS-SIL/ROBERT STADLER/RON ARAD/SATYENDRA PAKHALÉ/SEBASTIAN WRONG & RICHARD WOODS/ SHI JIANMIN/STEPHEN BURKS/STUDIO EDWARD VAN VLIET/STUDIO GORM/STUDIOILSE/STUDIO JOB/STUDIO MAKKINK & BEY/SYLVAIN WILLENZ/TAKASHI SATO/TJEP./TOM DIXON/TRANLOGUE ASSOCIATES INC/VINTA/WANNES ROYAARDS/WIS DESIGN

···

THIS IS THE DAY OF THE ENTERTAINERS, A GROUP OF DESIGNERS WHO NOT ONLY SEEM TO MOVE EFFORTLESSLY BETWEEN THE WORLDS OF ART AND DESIGN, BUT KNOW HOW TO MARKET THEMSELVES VERY WELL TOO.

Designers, said Ambra Medda, director of the Miami/Basel Design Fair in an interview, are the new rock stars. And given her successful fairs in Miami and Basel, where gallery-owners offered mainly prototypes and very limited series the international design jet set – according to Medda, "high-end limited edition design fair" – very little fault can be found with this statement. And given the almost frenzied rush to offer work by this very new genre of artist-designers in the auction houses of London and New York, and considering the number of companies who seem to feel comfortable in the role of publishing attention-grabbing avant-garde designs, Medda's words seem to be the very opposite of an exaggeration. The fact is that the new design art market, which has been active for only a few years, is able to offer something for everyone. Design is becoming art and art design, and on the design market at least the same rules apply as they do on the art market – on stage or under the auctioneer's hammer. And so? Is that what it is? Philippe Starck let us know recently that he had never created anything useful. And indeed it is scarcely possible to communicate the image of design as a discipline. When Jasper Morrison – certainly one of the key figures on the international design field – designs a chair that exists by the hundred already, it needs a particular intellectual effort see how it shows that design and indeed designers are needed today.

Marc Newson/Low Voronoi Shelf (white)

This is the day of the entertainers, a group of designers who not only seem to move effortlessly between the worlds of art and design, but who know how to market themselves very well too. Entertainers allow themselves to be guided by their market value alone, and that increases with every design that moves further away from our present understanding of design. The principle goes like this: something more can always be done. Breaking away from normal design manifestos is striking here in a number of ways. Entertainer design must be rare and costly. It must absolutely not be capable of being reproduced, and above all must infringe on aesthetic taboos. The first of these conditions is easy to meet, as proved by MARC NEWSON'S

marble furniture. Each of these stone objects, the Voronoi Shelf and the Extruded Chair, is made from a block of white Carrara marble. Given the size of the furniture, the number of appropriate blocks available is limited, and they take an enormous length of time to make, in short: the idea of a limited edition is built in from the outset. The objects command considerable sums at auction. But the number of top earners among designers who know how to instrumentalise the art market is still limited. Marc Newson is one of them, RON ARAD, the sculptor among designers, belongs here and so does Zaha Hadid, who when scaling her architecture down to the scale of products changes the materials as well – concrete becomes silver or a Swarowski crystal – and thus creates true luxury objects. But otherwise it is a market of the hopeful, and there are a lot

Ron Arad/Misfits

of those. For them the question of infringing on aesthetic taboos is a permanent challenge if they are to gain the blessing of the design art market.

Take JAIME HAYON, for example. He is a Spaniard who started his career as a designer in the pullover manufacturer Benetton's Fabrica thinktank, and in a very short period has become one of the most productive exponents of a style that is all its own, somewhere between art and design, and that is entirely comfortable with the notion of kitsch. It doesn't matter whether Hayon is designing shoes for campers, chandeliers for Nadia Swarovski's Crystal Palace Collection or bathtubs for ArtQuitect: Hayon loves spectacle, the common denominator for all his work. One of his most recent designs, commissioned by Bisazza for the Milan Furniture Fair 2008, is a three-dimensional illustration of an aircraft that

Jaime Hayon/Jet Set installation

was quite clearly built from the wrong materials and yet has the markedly childlike charm of a naïve idea of flying. At the end of the day, the old master Marc Newson had been taken with the idea of designing his own aircraft a few years previously. Of course this flying object was only an artistic item, and yet a very media-effective idea for the Cartier Foundation, without ever having to prove that it was able to fly.

The Swedish quartet called FRONT also offers great entertainment. Four designers who were mainly concerned to test boundaries in their work, whether in the typology of existing products, as in the "Animal thing" series for Moooi, in which naturalistic life-size casts of different animals – horses, pigs, rabbits – are used as supporting elements for lampshades or table-tops. They may explore new methods for the design process, or perhaps realise designs with the aid of Rapid Prototyping; here the designers try to turn hand sketches prepared in virtual space into real products, without constructing models or tools. The quartet provided their Shade series, launched in 2008 and consisting of furniture and tableware, with graphic decoration that made the products look like two-dimensional pencil drawings. Front plays with the idea of trompe l'oeil, a perspective optimised in the Renaissance, which is clearly an art category and had not previously been used in design. So it is no wonder that most of Front's commissions come from museums and galleries.

FRONT/Shade Vase

Holland, now as then, has to be seen as the key country for commuters between art and design. Dutch design training, which opened up an artistic view of design decoupled from industry earlier than other countries, produced a series of impressive designer personalities in past decades, and they helped to shape the concept of Dutch design. The Droog Design group, founded in 1993 more as a self-help institution, and now rather like a publishing house for the manifestation of a contemporary design concept that is spreading from Holland, committed itself to reviving craft techniques in association with Marcel Duchamp's ready-made idea. Droog collects, embroiders, crochets and pots, but on a large rather than a small scale: for example, everything MARCEL WANDERS touches has to be larger than life. This designer, who created one of Droog Design's most important successes at least in terms of public exposure in the form of his Knotted Chair, has devised a world of

Marcel Wanders/The Carved Chair

"Gothic Horrors" as art director of the Moooi concern that is best enjoyed to the sound of the Gothic Rock legend Sisters of Mercy. All the company's furniture seems inflated in some way, always larger than our standardised environment, as though it or its viewers is under the influence of hallucinatory drugs. The Moooi furniture is usually black, and constantly quotes Baroque forms and decorative worlds. It looks like the silhouettes used in Chinese shadow plays, popular above all in the opium dens of the dying Chinese Empire.

And the Dutch school – so it would seem – tirelessly produces young designers who are able to set themselves up in the intermediate world as artist-designers. Take the STUDIO JOB practise, for example: both professionally and privately, Job Smeets and Nynke Tynagel are a couple who seem to entirely at home in the Duchamp tradition of lending aesthetic quality to banal everyday objects. They developed their "Home Work" series in 2007 for the Groningen Museum and the Moss Gallery in New York. Their subtitle rightly defines this collection of bronze pots, stools and lanterns, stacked to form seven individual oversize towers, as

Studio Job/Homework

"Domestic Totems and Tableaux". The fact is that what they have stacked up were fetishes, for domestic use. Moss also demonstrated in New York this year that stacking objects is perhaps the most powerful recurrent motif in Studio Job's work. An exhibition by the Amsterdam Rijksmuseum in the gallery showed work by Studio Job and other Dutch designers – including Hella Jongerius, Jurgen Bey and Alexander van Slobbe – who addressed the old technique of pyramids made up of Delft porcelain vases, a technique for stacking different bodies that became very popular in the 17th century, when it was called a Makkum pyramid.

Stacking as a Dutch readymade design motif can also be found in the work of another Dutch design star. In 2004, MAARTEN BAAS translated his finals project for the Eindhoven Academy into a different dimension, again at the invitation of Murray Moss in New York. Baas worked on pieces of furniture he had found with a Bunsen burner, so that all the different finds became something like a collection of burned furniture that developed an aesthetic that was all its own as a result of its uniformly black and porous surface. Moss invited Baas to char design classics like Ettore Sottsass's Carlton Regal or the Macintosh chair, then presented a "Where there's smoke" exhibition in his gallery that successfully put visitors into a strangely revolutionary mood in relation to the design establishment.

Maarten Baas/SCULPT drawer

But Maarten Baas shows his ability to stack things in an interesting way in his China Project in particular. This was his name for his first co-operation with the Contrast Gallery in Shanghai, in which he presented furniture installations that Chinese woodworkers had implemented from his designs. The central element in the exhibition in the autumn of 2008 is his "Chinese Objects Object", a pyramid of Chinese furniture – chairs, tables and bureaux – that Baas stacked one on top of the other as usual. Baas seems to take pleasure in the absurd in all his works, and this applies particularly to his current work "The Chankley Bore", for Established & Sons. "The Chankley Bore" is a series of storehouse furniture that seems to have emerged from Goethe's Sorcerer's Apprentice in the 1940 Walt Disney version: these a comic-like bodies with souls that keep starting to move, and could develop into uncontrollable nightmares for anyone who uses them.

And in fact, nightmare does capture part of the effect the Entertainers achieve with their work. Another part can mean inspiration or pleasure. But anyway the Entertainers have succeeded in attracting a great deal of public interest in design as a discipline towards their work. Essentially they produce work for museums, but we shall have to wait and see how quickly their work there finds its way from the display areas into the archives.

MAARTEN BAAS
SCULPT
1 Cupboard
2 Drawer
3 Armchair
7 Dining chair
Influenced by the spontaneity, crude-
ness and primal character of miniature
sketch models, Baas sculpted functional furniture. Every part of the production process, such as welding, grinding,
veneering and even the production of
hinges and handles was done by hand.

4,5,6 The Chankley Bore storage
Named for a line from a nonsense poem,
these fantastical storage containers
represent Baas' attempt to work outside
conventional furniture templates.

1

4

5

2

3

6

7

1

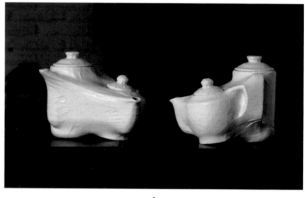

2

3

COMMITTEE
Mr and Mrs Richardson
1 Bamboo lamp
A light that combines the organic shapes of bamboo with a modernist base by uniting them under a high-gloss surface. Each lamp has a unique pull switch handle that dangles like an ear-ring beneath its shade, encouraging the user to untie the knot and replace it with a different object.

PEPE HEYKOOP
2 Tape Pot teapot
Found beside each other in a secondhand shop, these teapots were bound together with layers of tape to become a tapepot – recycling forms as well as material.

SEBASTIAN WRONG & RICHARD WOODS
3 The WrongWoods chest of drawers

FRONT
Soft Wood furniture
Sofa, bench and chair upholstered in a
textile printed with enlarged wood grain.

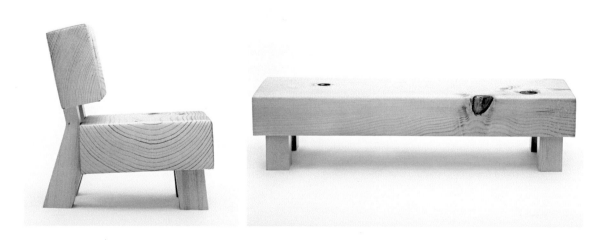

BRAM BOO
Pages 95, 202–204, 213

Belgian designer Bram Boo claims to design surprising objects – and does. His austerely simple seating, storage and tables are hard-working objects – reconfigurable, multitasking – with severe angles, clean lines and hollow appendages.

After school, Boo assisted artist Bram Bogart before beginning to design furniture for his own use and taking night classes in carpentry, metal and polyester fabrication. Following graduation in industrial design from the Royal Academy of Art in Hasselt, Begium (for which city he was later commissioned to plan a public footpath), 2002 marked a watershed in Boo's design, which thereafter became both increasingly sure-handed, original and playful. The double-skinned Tete á Tete is a table that can slough off its outer layer to form a table-bench combination. (FELD now manufactures Boo's similar Etcetera picnic table.) Use Me's two obtuse plywood L's can be slid into each other to form a bench with an integrated desktop and seat. The Daltons, three chairs of increasing size, can be stood on their heads and leaned together to become both a ladder and a bookcase. With its hollow hide, is Loch Ness a storage element or a desk and stool? Anubis does look like a proud canine god at rest but actually is a two-part veneered ply piece that can be pushed together to form a chaise longue with a cantilevered surface that could be a sidetable or, turned around, serve as a writing desk and seat with armchair. The lacquered plywood Gypsy Things includes several tables and chairs that resemble periscopes and cartoon quadripeds with duct-like voids for storage. The naked plywood swivel chair Paparazzi features generous pockets that make it as much seating as workspace.

Boo, then, is the equivalent of a cartoonist, populating the world with gentle creatures whose long necks and rectilinear flanks fill homes and offices with friendly, and highly functional, furniture.

1 Paparazzi task chair
  An office chair with storage bins.
  Combining functions in single pieces
  of furniture is typical of Boo and gives
  each piece strong character.

2 Backstage cupboard
  Backstage is a cupboard with external
  storage elements.

3 Loch Ness storage/desk/seating

1

2

3

1

5

2

3

4

6

1 Anubis chaise longue
Seating that doubles as both work and relaxation space.

2 Chica table
This table features two additional functions: storage space and seating.

3 Chico table
A table that also serves as seat and bar counter.

4 Lazy desk
This work surface contains storage elements that Boo placed strategically and unconventionally in order to give the object more personality.

5 Chico table with El Loco, Mambo, Gigolo and Django chairs
Pieces of the "Gypsy Things" collection. Like gypsies, says the designer, each objects "has a strong personality: inventive, poetic, proud and full of irony."

6 Matrioshka stackable chairs
Like the Russian dolls that nest neatly one within other, these chairs are compact in order to be easily stored.

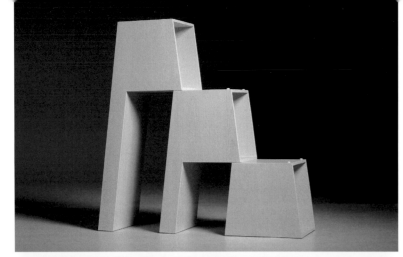

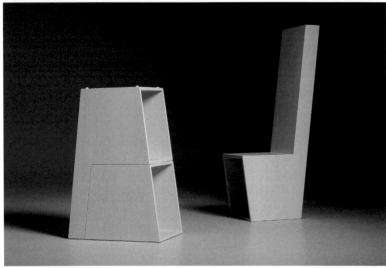

BRAM BOO

1 The Daltons seating/bookase/ladder
   This trio of chairs morphs into a bookcase or ladder.

3 Salsa seating
   A piece of furniture that provides the
   opportunity to socialise, rest or work.

JOOST VAN BLEISWIJK

2 Outlines furniture

3

FRÉDÉRIC RUYANT
1 Tribu tables

KATRIN SONNLEITNER
2 Kommode & Co. table
Sonnleitner imagines, and creates, objects that coexist so closely that they take on symbiotic or parasitic relationships as if they were creatures that have gone through a process of evolution. This project examines how the relationships we force upon objects like a commode, a lamp, a doily and a carpet influence and inspire the design of new objects, resulting in a group of small hybrid commodes.

3 Moving Habits drawers

1

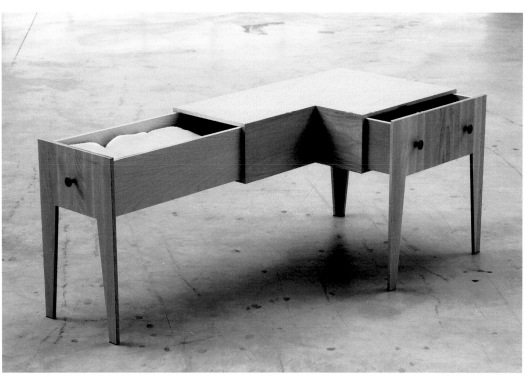

2

3

**PER EMANUELSSON &
BASTIAN BISCHOFF**
1,3,4 Surveillance floor lamp

WIS DESIGN
2   Dot floor lamp
     Dot's light switch is inspired by a
     pearl necklace.

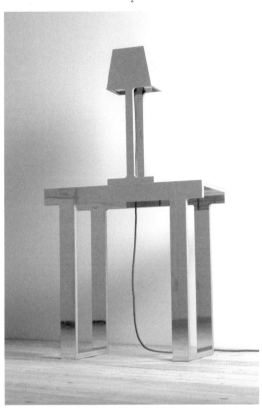

2

1

3
4

LIFEGOODS
ECAL/Olivier Burgisser
1 Bedside table
Bedside table with sides made of PVC
bristles to hide electrical grips and cables.

WANNES ROYAARDS
2 Bedside table
A table designed for use in the Lloyd
Hotel Amsterdam.

WIS DESIGN
3 Proper pendant light
The interior brass net resembles
a petticoat, which is concealed by the
plywood shade and swooshes around the
bulb to create a diffuse, warm light.

VINTA
Kohei Okamoto+Toshitaka Nakamura
4 AfterDark lamp
Savour bedtime with a pool of chocolate on your nightstand.

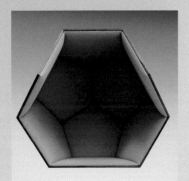

ROBERT STADLER
Pages 208, 267

Perhaps it's because Robert Stadler lives in the world of ideas that he works all over the map. The Vienna-born artist divides his time between Paris and Rio de Janeiro, happily annihilating the boundaries between, and hierarchies of, art and design, highbrow and low.

Trained at the Istituto Europeo di Design in Milan and ENSCI/Les Ateliers in Paris, he became one of the co-founders of the quirky Radi Designers in 1992 before going solo (although he continues to collaborate with Radi). Created as a solo project in 2005, Stadler's limited-edition mural-clock, 24H Linda uses an LCD screen and epoxy-coated metal housing to create a large light-box photograph that also serves as a timepiece. It takes time, however, for the viewer to discover the hands of the clock within the image in order to read it.

In 2006, Stadler designed a limited-edition perfume diffuser to contain a scent created by Calice Becker for Quest that was produced by Fondation Bernardaud. Burning Desire, made from double-fired, partially enameled, molded porcelain, was made for the exhibition "Essences Insensées" during the Paris Parcours Saint-Germain as a three-dimensional translation of Becker's fragrance. The object was fabricated in two sections, one of which held plaster granules infused with the scent, which was then diffused through an aperture in the vessel throughout the room.

In 2007, Stadler christened his one-way "mirror-oracle" Carole. Embedded with clever electronics, Carole displays aphorisms and proverbs through the looking glass in answer to a viewer's query. Leaning on the old, low-tech fortune teller trope instead of any tricky mechanism, Stadler allows viewers to tell their own fortunes: because the phrases are random and not targeted to individual users, their very lack of specificity imbues them with mystery, encouraging users to invent a connection between the statement and their own lives. It's easy to predict that Stadler will continue to keep the design industry (and art world?) entertained.

Pentaphone microarchitecture
Pentaphone offers private space within a public space that can isulate the user from ambient noise.

KATRIN SONNLEITNER

1 Immöbel chest of drawers
As a storage unit, the chest of drawers is not very easy to move around. Since it was placed in the bedroom with its back against the wall, many smaller objects like lamps, vases or doilies have populated its top and reduced it to a pedestal for life's souvenirs. Immöbel rebels against this by abandoning its accustomed shape in favour of a new arrangement that isn't as easy to use as a display surface. Users must develop new strategies of using their furniture and reconsider their behaviour towards the objects that surround them.

STUDIO GORM
Wonhee Jeong

2 Platform bed
A platform bed shaped like a typical Korean house with porch, stoop and a movable lamp. The canopy is made from modular structural blankets.

3 Shed/Shelf storage unit
A cabinet in the form of a doll's house for grownups to keep things organised within a small apartment and to remind users to not take life too seriously.

1

2

3

1

CRISTIAN ZUZUNAGA

1 Pixelated fabric

Zuzunaga sees the city as a gravita-
tional force that draws people towards
it, creating a diverse environment that
fosters symbiotic relationships to be
forged between people and elements
of the urban environment. In April 2006,
while studying at the Royal College of
Art, the designer's dissertation research
led him to Shanghai where he studied
Supermodern architecture, global cities
and the pixel, which he sees as the icon
of our era, and which he celebrates in
this upholstery textile.

JANTZE BROGÅRD ASSHOFF

2 Field sofa

A sofa with unique details such as
chunky, embroidered buttons inspired
by traditional Swedish folk costumes.

2

1

2

WIS DESIGN, JANTZE BROGÅRD ASSHOFF & MALIN LUNDMARK

1 Camp Site Berns exhibition
Camp Site is an exhibition and an experience put together in 2007 by a collective consisting of six young Swedish designers. Camp Site will be a reccurring event, during which the designers will set up temporary "camps." At the inaugural Camp Site Berns the collective redesigned a bar and lounge.

WIS DESIGN

2 Twine table
Twine is a series of tables inspired by one of mankind's most simple inventions: the button. The tabletop is an over-size button pierced by metal wire "thread" that forms its base.

FORM US WITH LOVE

3,5 Button pouf
Upholstered seating in various diameters dressed in waste cloth from the textile industry.

JANTZE BROGÅRD ASSHOFF

4 Party pouf
A pouf dressed in soft knitted fabric.

3

4

5

211

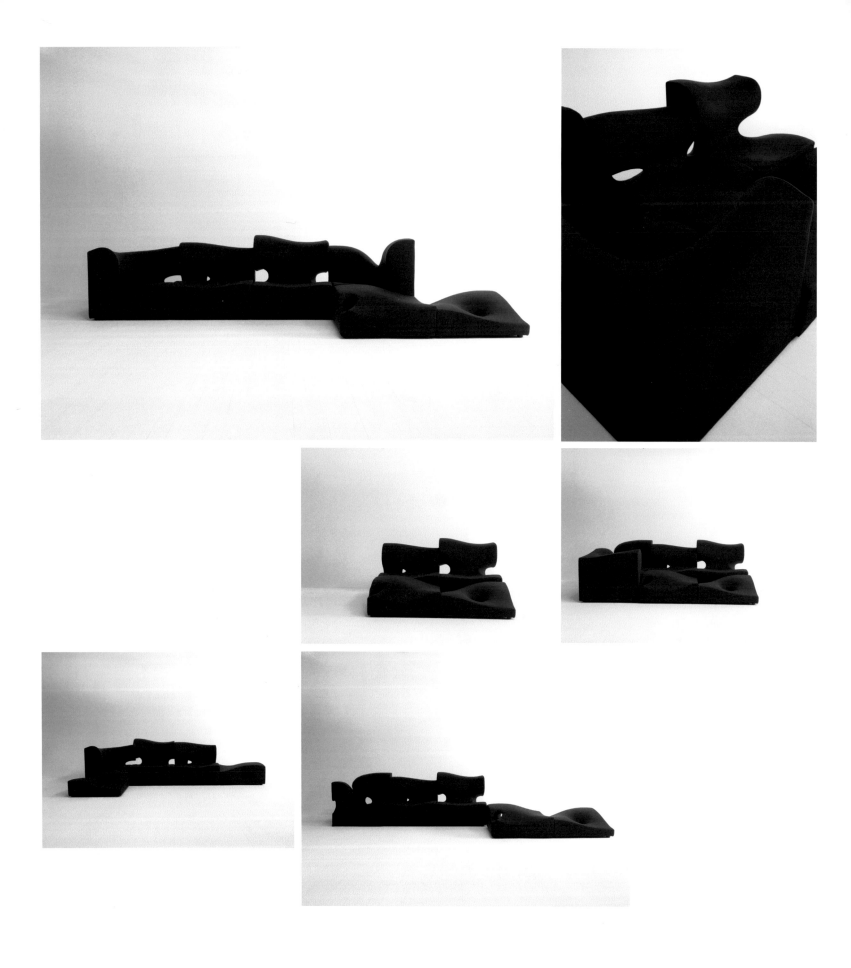

RON ARAD
Misfits modular sofa

READYMADE PROJECTS
Stephen Burks
Pleats sofa
Designed from the upholstery inwards
in response to the tactility of the fabric,
Pleats focuses attention on the sensations
elicited by sitting on a particular textile
Artisanal kilt makers in the U.K. were
sourced to develop the innovative hand-
pleated fabric.

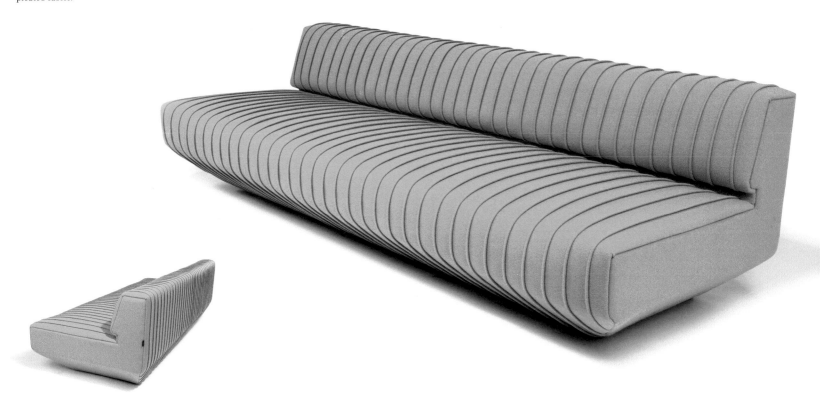

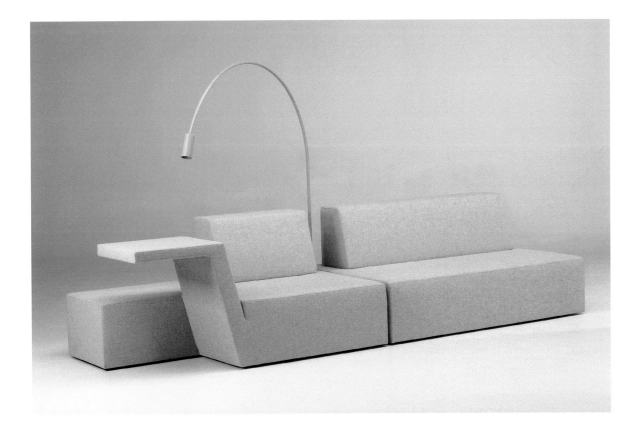

BRAM BOO
Oasis couch with lamp
A couch consisting of two reconfigurable seating elements. On one side users
can work on a labtop or recline as if on a
chaise longue.

1

MARCEL WANDERS
1   The Carved Chair
2   The Clock Chair
3,4 Naval Brass Collection
    A collection consisting of lamps, candle-
    sticks and bowls.

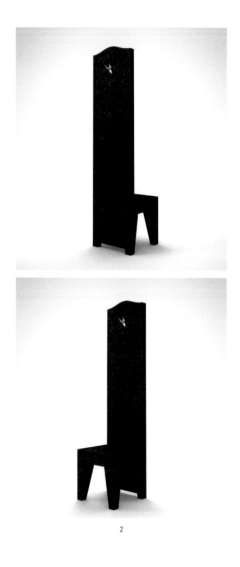

2

3

4

SYLVAIN WILLENZ

1   Torch Bunch 10 chandelier
2   Torch Series: Large Cone/Small Round/
    Small Cone lamps
    Made from a moulded textured plastic,
    Torch can be suspended from the ceil-
    ing in single units, arranged in clusters
    of 10 or 20, or used individually on a
    tabletop or in the corner of a room.
    Inspired by the silhouette of a typical
    handheld torch or car headlight. "This
    is how I like to think of objects," says
    Willenz. "What would they be like
    as shadows?"

MATHIAS BENGTSSON

3   MAC couch
    The Modular Aluminium Concept couch
    is formed from 34 modular sections of
    extruded chrome-coated aluminium.

ANNA JAMES

4   Erte dressing table
    Inspiration for this piece came from
    an Harper's Bazar cover by Erte from
    the 1920s.

215

KJELLGREN KAMINSKY
ARCHITECTURE
Fredrik Kjellgren & Joakim Kaminsky

Remember when architects designed everything from furniture to the master plans of cities? Joakim Kaminsky and Fredrik Kjellgren still do. After winning an international competition to design a dance hall in 2006, the friends opened KjellgrenKaminsky Architecture in Gothenburg, Sweden. Between them they have the design DNA of firms such as Wingardhs and UN-studio, Ben Van Berkel & Caroline Bos, but their furniture design is uniquely their own, the product of two unusual and articulate imaginations.

In 2008, the architects put out their Pirate Baroque series, including a stool, lounge and stackable chairs in lacquered wood and steel covered with a show-stopping blue fabric. To create the turned-wood seating, they "pirated" the styles of forgotten chairs found in junk shops and in their great grandmothers' parlours.

This followed the debut of Kjellgren's Praline Noir Black Velvet bench for Materia. The design recalls his grandmother's home, which was chock full of art and design, he recounts, "fancy cushions with glittering buttons, shimmering silk, plush that felt rough to the touch, handles draped with tassels that gently swung aside when you entered the room, mirrors, carpets, sculptures. Everything had a story, but not always a purpose." It was a place where the historical and cultural value of the furniture was superceded by its functionality.

Praline was actually a sequel to Kjellgren's A Pompous Fat Armchair. Pompous Fat is a recliner as luridly seductive as a naughty stage set out of the TV show The Tudors. It squats on steel legs and is made up of discs upholstered in various black Fanny Aronsen fabrics tufted with vintage buttons. "The clash between the things I like and the things I dislike is the leading theme of 'My Pompous Fat Armchair,'" explains Kjellgren. "The reclining easy chair has become synonymous with poor taste. I found that I hated to look at it but found it very comfortable to sit in. I had come out. Out from the dark, pompous furniture closet." And so should we.

A Pompous Fat Armchair
An expressive piece of furniture, this reclining armchair represents the designer's exploration of a type of furniture he discovered that he simultaneously liked and disliked.

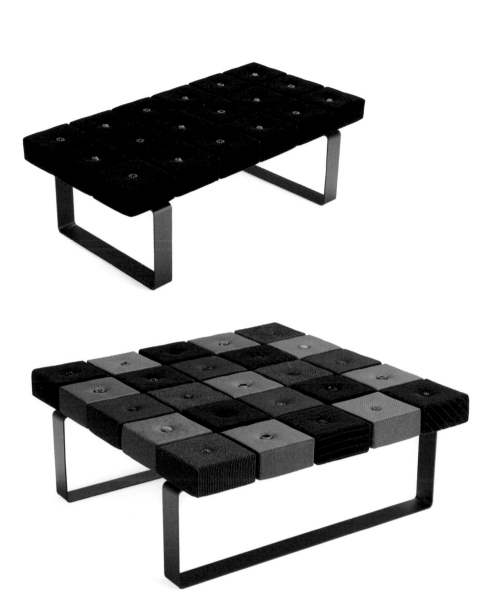

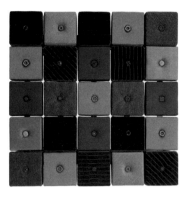

Praline Noir seating
A celebration of objects that have a story but not a function anchored around fancy cushions that symbolise a historical, but not practical, object. Two seats, Praline Noir 6x3 and Praline Noir 5x5, made from Fanny Aronsen fabrics, unique soutache, metal and plastic vintage buttons, prompt the simple question that permeated the entire project: can one sit on a fancy cushion?

1   SOFA lamp
Inspired by the iconic Chesterfield sofa, this lamp takes its familiar aesthetic out of context, creating a lamp that communicates all the social values of this emblematic piece of furniture.

1

F.AKASAKA EDITIONS
Fernando Akasaka
2   FA32 "Cowboy Junkie" stool
A stool whose seat is made from a jumping saddle of premium French leather and featuring large knee and thigh rolls, hide-covered pads, cut back head and stuffed panels. The FA32 stool is stamped, signed, numbered and accompanied by a certificate of authenticity.

NIKA ZUPANC
3   Feather duster
A re-interpretation of one of the household's worn icons and part of Zupanc's La Femme et La Maison collection. This assortment of completely ordinary and sometimes bizarre objects, which belong to (or used to belong to) every home, has been dressed up with high-tech materials and a fetish aesthetic, the objects are given new meaning. In a sociological sense, the feather duster has been both a tool and even a symbol of the waning patriarchy and a bond that tied women to the home. Now it becomes a playful toy of modern consumers, both male and female.

ARIK BEN SIMHON
4   Mickey Max armchair
Bladerunner meets Mickey Mouse in a tufted armchair.

NIKA ZUPANC
5   Unfaithful dressing table
Part of the La Femme et La Maison collection as an ultimately feminine and unjustly neglected piece of furniture. In the original concept, Zupanc wanted the table to feature an oval LED display, an Internet connection and small camera instead of a mirror, giving it a technological value that would earn it a place amongst modern objects.

6   Maid chair
Confess, urges Zupanc. You say never, but you always wanted to know how it feels to be trussed up in laces. Maid's shape traces the sensual curves of the ideal feminine body.

3

2

4

5

6

PHIL CUTTANCE
1 Cloud City chandelier

STUDIO EDWARD VAN VLIET
Edward van Vliet
2 Royal BB chandelier

BARLAS BAYLAR
3 Atlantis chandelier
The concept behind Atlantis was to
make something soft and organic out of
metal, which is traditionally not associated with softness.

DANIEL BECKER
4 Tee-Licht light
Tee-Licht originated from the idea to
design a Ready Made, using convetion-
al bulbs which imitate the light of
a small candle in a poetic way. The contrast between the shining exterior
and the empty, dark interior is what
Becker sought to emphasise.

JOOST VAN BLEISWIJK
5 Single Cut vases
By drawing a vase shape on a piece of cardboard, and folding the board along this line,
a new vase shape arises. Created in an edition of 100 unique vases.

FRÉDÉRIC RUYANT
6 O(d), O(r), O(z) vases

3

4

5

6

STUDIO JOB
Job Smeets & Nynke Tynagel
Robber Baron furniture

Robber Baron tales of power, corruption, art, and industry, cast in bronze by Studio Job, is a suite of five cast-bronze furnishings to be offered in a limited edition of five, exclusive to Moss. Cast with precision mechanical movements where required, incorporating deeply carved iconographic reliefs, with areas highly polished, gilded, or patinated, the pieces are highly crafted.

1   Table
    A patinated bronze "factory", whose architecture is derived from interpretations of various early 20th-century works, including the AEG factory of Peter Behrens and the Battersea Power Station in London. The four chimneys produce a "polluted cloud" of polished bronze, which becomes the open-work tabletop.
2   Mantel clock
    A patinated bronze pedestal clock supported by gilded oil barrels atop a model of the Florentine Galleria degli Uffizi with Robber Baron reliefs. The dial of the clock is inspired by London's Big Ben, circled by a futile railway running endless circles on a rocky landscape. The clock face can be shut with cast bronze stable doors. On top of the clock sits a Neo-Classical "dream house", partially shrouded by a cloud.
3   Jewel safe
    A patinated bronze safe with a Jack-in-the-Box popping up out of its craggy crown. Its polished bronze head is coloured with oil-based pigments, highlighting the collar, nose and other features. The lock mechanism is operated by turning the clown's nose, and the door hinge employs a ball bearing mechanism.
4   Standing lamp
    A patinated bronze floor lamp in which three important icons of architecture - the Parthenon, the Empire State Building and Saint Peter's Basilica - merge into one. The Zeppelin docked at the pinnacle symbolises technological failure, and refers to the Empire State Building, the top spire of which was originally intended as a mooring for airships. When illuminated, the hundreds of windows glow, diffused by a hand-blown frosted glass interior. The light bulbs can be changed by lifting the polished bronze cloud.
5   Cabinet
    A polished bronze cabinet with black patinated bomb crater and gilded reliefs, inspired by a 17th-century armoire by André-Charles Boulle, in the Wallace Collection, London. The heavy doors are fully functional thanks to a ball-bearing mechanism.

1

2

3

4

5

STUDIO JOB
Job Smeets & Nynke Tynagel
Homework objects

A suite of eight works: seven heroic compositions in bronze, glass, and wood plus one monumental wall mirror. Each piece is offered in a limited edition of five, exclusive to Moss. Part domestic utility, part heroic sculpture, these precious handwrought common household objects – including fully-functional cooking pots, stools, lanterns, and coal bins – handsculpted first in wax in exalted proportions, and then rendered in polished bronze and placed upon aged wooden pedestals reminiscent of sacred statuary or palatial historical busts, define the term "oxymoron" and cast to the winds the traditional approach to both sculptural as well as design practice. Circumventing the Duchampian argument surrounding what is, and what is not art, Studio Job does not employ "readymades" – ordinary manufactured objects which, as defined by Duchamp, are then elevated to the dignity of a work of art – but, rather, creates through sanctioned classical "artistic processes" these elegantly rendered "portraits" of anonymous 20th century industrial designs. The work challenges the art market's half-hearted acknowledgement of the sculptural or artistic qualities of industrially produced utilitarian objects. Like certain so-called "functional" yet highly expressive works before them, created by artist/designers such as Ettore Sottsass, Shiro Kuramata, Gaetano Pesce and Bruno Munari, these artifacts are hybrids, both object and objet d'art.

STUDIO JOB
Job Smeets & Nynke Tynagel
Collection FARM
During Salone del Mobile Milano 2008, Design House (directed by Li Edelkoort) presented an installation called "FARM". The show marked a return to the rural as a design subject and depicts humble stable equipment, a spade and fork, milk pitchers and pails, cooking pots and a frying pan that also doubles as a mirror. Now that the farmers of the world will clothe, feed and fuel us, a far-reaching movement will trigger designers to revisit folk and farm mentalities to blend rural and urban style. The exhibition consisted of 24 bronze works and six pieces of pallissander furniture which evoked the archetypal artefacts of Germany, Flanders and The Netherlands.

JAIME HAYON
1 Tudor chairs

STUDIO EDWARD VAN VLIET
Edward van Vliet
2 Lazslo chair

NIKA ZUPANC
1 Lolita floor Lamp
2 Lolita table Lamp

BAS VAN DER VEER
3 One table with integrated vase

STUDIO MAKKINK & BEY
Rianne Makkink & Jurgen Bey
4 Cleaning-Beauty-Bathtub
Handcrafted in porcelain with a sculpted lid to keep the water warm and hand-drawn bathers and swimming fish ornamenting interior surfaces.

1

2

3

4

5

6

F. AKASAKA DESIGN
Fernando Akasaka

1   FA10 stool/side table

2   FA29 table or floor lamp
    A lamp providing diffused light.

3   FA19 stool/side table
4   FA1 bench
5   FA5 stool/side table
6   FA11 side table
7   FA27 lamp
8   FA31 table lamp

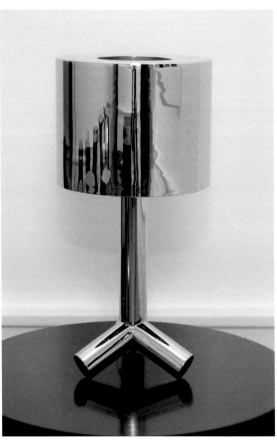

7

8

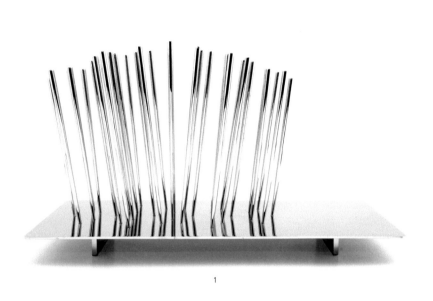

F. AKASAKA DESIGN
Fernando Akasaka

1   FA17 magazine rack
2   FA16 magazine rack
3   FA7 stool/side table
4   FA4 stool/side table
5   FA2 chair
6   FA22 chair

231

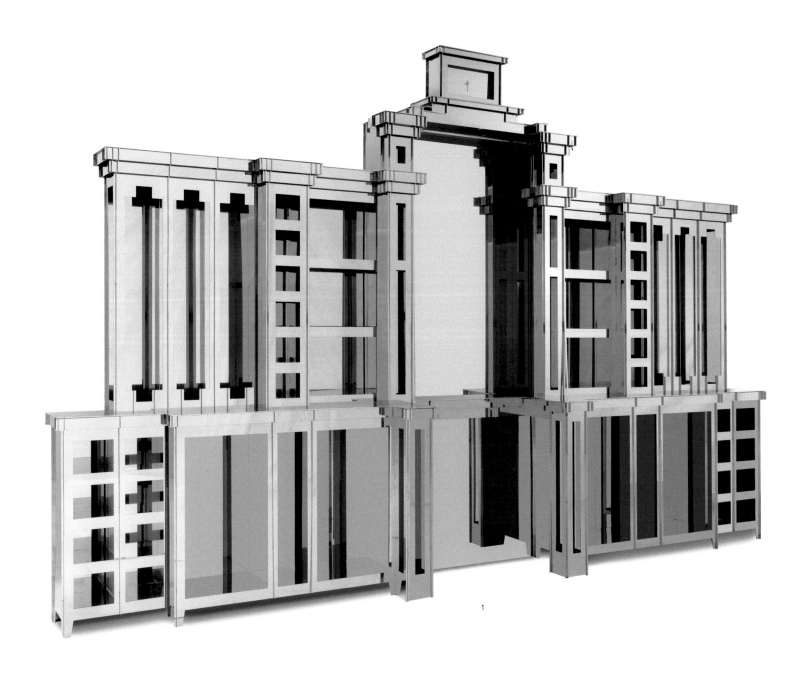

JOOST VAN BLEISWIJK
No Screw No Glue collection
1 Wall Cabinet
   Cabinet as wall, or the wall as an entire cabinet. This ambitious piece combines fireplace, altar and storage unit and is an effort to make a definitive amalgam of historical cabinet designs that encompasses "all meanings of wall decoration," says van Bleiswijk.
2 High Cabinet XL

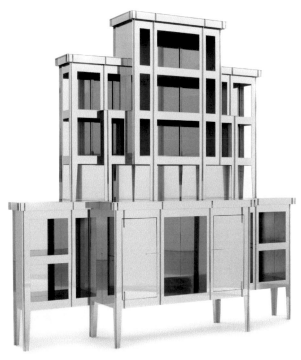

JOOST VAN BLEISWIJK
No Screw No Glue Collection
1 Little Clock
2 Candelabrum
   This candelabrum holds five candles,
   and is inspired by 17th-century can-
   dlesticks and table settings where
   light and the entire atmosphere of a
   table was generated by silver cande-
   labra. Due to the careful detailing of
   the object, light is reflected off more
   than 140 facets.
3 Trophy
4 Little Lamp
5 Chess game
   A game board made up of 689 seper-
   ate hand-polished elements.

6 Roberval balance

7 Compose Series Treasury
   In the Compose series, Bleiswijk acts
   like a little boy playing with wood-
   blocks. Composing shapes with solid
   pieces of wenge wood, he finally fixes
   them by casting pewter in routed slots.

1

2

3

4

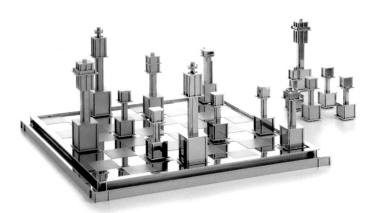

5

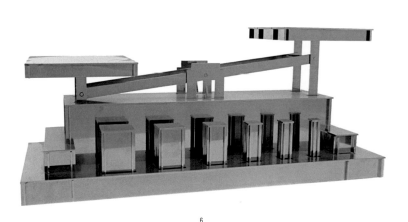

6

7

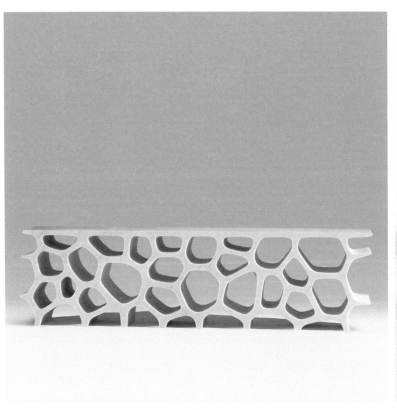

1

2

MARC NEWSON
1 Low Voronoi shelf
2 Extruded Table 3
3 Carbon Fibre chair

3

1

2

3

4

5

F. AKASAKA DESIGN
Fernando Akasaka
1   FA30 table / floor lamp

BARBER OSGERBY
2   Zero-In coffee table
The 12 pieces in the edition are made
from aluminium sheet, which is formed
by hand in several sections and welded
together to create the inner and outer
walls of the table by craftsmen who traditionally work in high-end sports car
restoration. The welded joints are worked
by hand until they are no longer visible.

3   Iris 1500 low table
The IRIS series features five tables, each
with its own specific colour spectrum.
Iris 1500 comes in grey tones and was
inspired by the firm's use of various types
of colour charts in its day-to-day work.
1500 is constructed from a single geometric component repeated 60 times to form
a tessellated ring. Each component is machined from solid anodised aluminium.

4   Double Bottle table
5   Bottle table
The Bottle table is made entirely from
Calacata or Marquinia marble.

BARLAS BAYLAR
Knight Base dining table with Atlantis
chandelier and Eaton chair

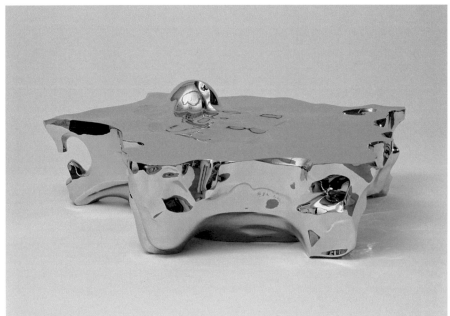

1

2

4

3

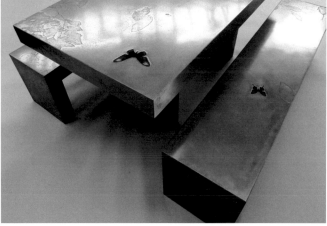

5

GABRIELLE AMMANN // DESIGNER'S GALLERY
Shi Jianmin
1   Coffee table/stool

BASED UPON
Giorgio Gurioli
2   The Kundalini Hara chair

GABRIELLE AMMANN // DESIGNER"S GALLERY
Satyendra Pakhalé
3   Alu Rocking chair

BASED UPON
Giorgio Gurioli
4   A Coffee Table No.1
    The parched desert, a symbol of poverty,
    is recreated in platinum as a statement of
    luxury. But the crack, found in much of the
    studio's work, represents an archetypal di-
    vide between the two.

5   Butterfly table and benches

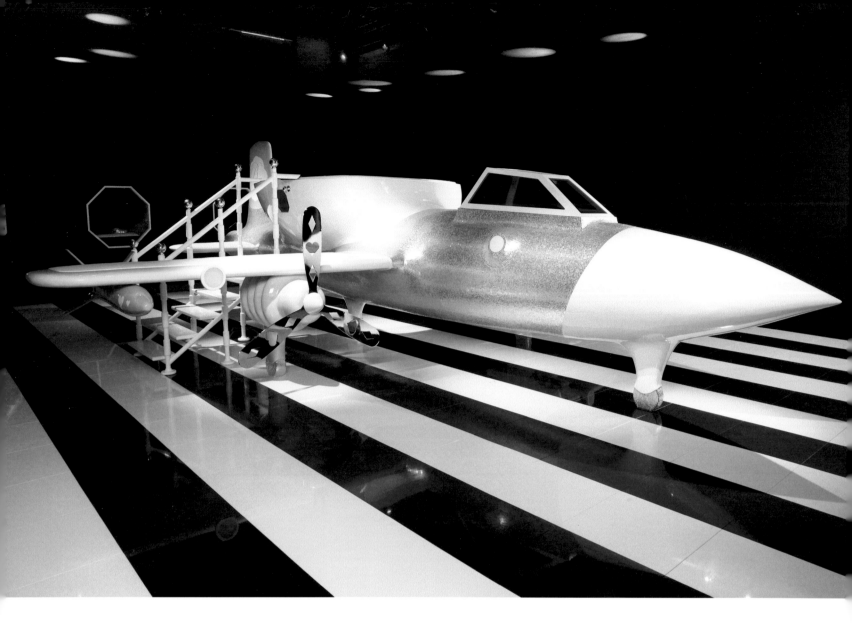

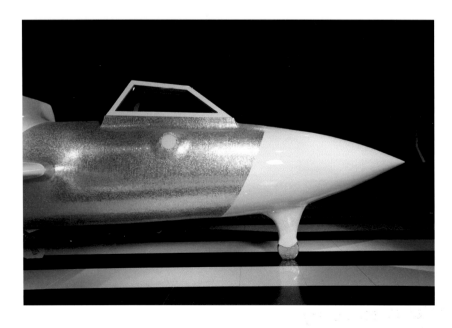

JAIME HAYON
Jet Set installation

1

2

TOM DIXON

1 Fat Spot light
The pure copper used is a vacuum me-
talised film, only microns thick, on the
interior of a polycarbonate sphere.

2 Copper Shades

3 CU29 armchair
A limited edition version of an expanded
polystyrene chair given away by Dixon in
Trafalgar Square in the autumn of 2006.
This vacuum-metallised copper version
was sold at Moss to finance the giveaway.

4 Beat vessels
These unpolished brass floor vases are
handcrafted using the traditional, rapidly
vanishing skills of Indian master craftsmen.

3

4

1

2

3

4

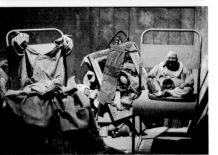

5

BASED UPON

1   The Vitra Panton chair

2   Number One object
    Carved out of polystyrene and shea-
    thed in a fine coat of metal, No. 1 was
    suspended on invisible wires during an
    exhibition to make viewers wonder if
    it might fall on them at any moment,
    crushing them with their own longing.

3   Taking the Piss £100,000 pissoir
    A play on Duchamp's pissoir which,
    when signed, became art and expo-
    nentially more valuable, this version
    incorporates a price tag instead of
    a signature and is aimed at the person
    who wants to pay £100,000 for it, not
    the £3000 that it was worth the day
    it was made. Now recognised as art, its
    value is also rising towards the price
    in its title.

4   The Breathing Box object
    This solid iron cube appears to breathe,
    representing the moment in life when
    all desire drains away, leaving only the
    longing to draw one more breath.

5   Desire installation
    An imagined alchemist's house seems
    to promise all that one could desire but
    delivers only rust in this installation
    about desire.

1

2

3

4

GABRIELLE AMMANN // DESIGNER'S GALLERY
Johanna Grawunder

1 Switch furniture
A movable interior element with a mirror on
one side and glass shelves on the other.

2 VuVanity furniture
Furniture for the bar or vanity

3 Splits bench/light
A movable bench with LED lighting in eight
colours.

ARIK BEN SIMHON
4 Grand Luxus light
Perspex neon light

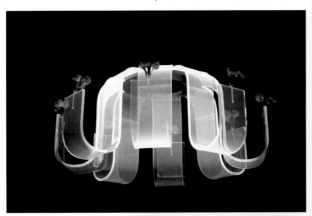

1

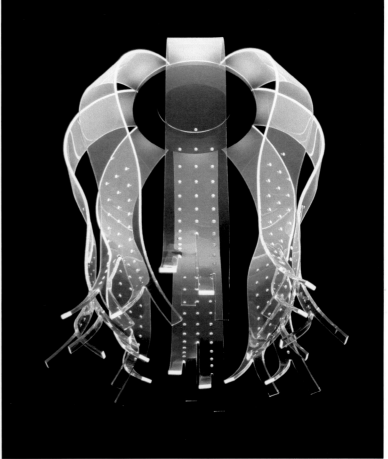

5

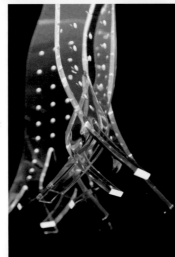

2

3

6

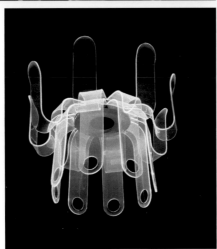

4

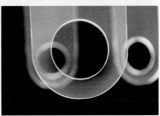

7

TRANLOGUE ASSOCIATES
AirLUCE chandeliers
1 Jellyfish
2,5 Bellflower
3 AirPlants
4,7 Fruits Flower
6 Anemone
The intention when designing this lighting was that it would be used in buildings that require a sophisticated, relaxing atmosphere. These pieces provide environmental lighting that can heighten the subdued character of an interior. The fixtures use an invisible and eco-friendly LED light source in the form of surface-emitting acrylic boards that emit light while retaining their transparency. This type of illumination is easy on the eyes because the light from an LED enters one edge of the acrylic while its source remains hidden from view.

KONSTANTIN GRCIC INDUSTRIAL DESIGN
Lunar chandelier

1

MIN CHEN

1   Airfall partition
The plastic of the Airfall partition is
so sensitive that it uses indoor air cur-
rents to rotate.

FORM US WITH LOVE

2   Construction Lamp
A 21st-century take on the traditional
work lamp.

FOR USE

3   Numen-Light objects
Face to face mirrors provide theoreti-
cally infinite reflections. Because the
designers made the boxes from "spy-
glass" or one-way mirror (typically used
for peep shows and police line-ups),
the viewer can view this infinity from
outside. The interior of each box is
defined by luminous strips positioned
along the inner edges of the parallel
epiped, creating an illusion of an end-
less grid of light. These pieces also
served as case studies for a stage set
for Dante's Inferno designed by For Use.

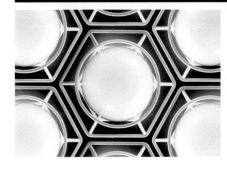
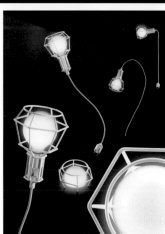

2

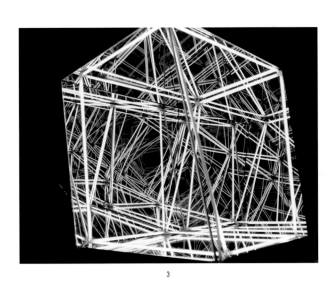

3

1

2

3

4

5

FRONT
1,2 Shade vase
3 Shade cup
4 Shade plate
5 Shade table
Two-dimensional sketches of furniture, hand-drawn by Front, were
brought to life in three dimensions and displayed at the Milan
furniture fair in 2008.

ANNA JAMES
Verona wardrobe
A graffiti-clad Rococo wardrobe, inspired by the house in Verona supposedly inhabited by the model for Shakespeare's character Juliet, the walls of which are covered in declarations of love by fans of the legend of "Romeo and Juliet."

PHILIP EDIS
1 Let Loose valet stand
A valet stand, upholstered with screen-printed textile, the back leg of which can fold up when not in use.

PHIL CUTTANCE
2 Fantasy Fantasy chair
A chair upholstered with a world of she-beasts, otherworldly landscapes, and a noble barbarian. It consists of a seat, back and a pair of arms, all easily assembled with connector bolts.

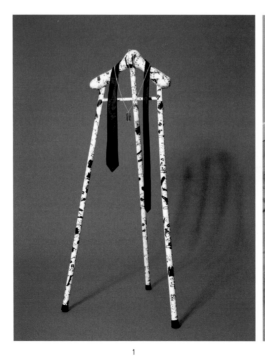

1

2

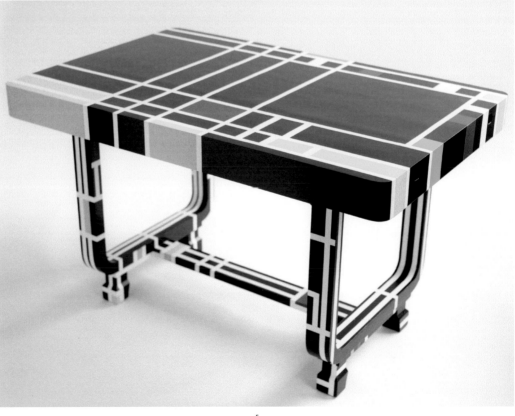

ANNA JAMES

1 Granny Takes a Trip secretary
   This piece is an original 1920s writing
   bureau made of oak in the Art Deco
   style. James was inspired by the famous
   boutique "Granny Takes a Trip" in the
   Kings Road London in the 1960s.

2 Hercule desk

3 Romeo and Juliet bedside tables
   "Romeo and Juliet" graffiti-clad bedside
   tables, inspired by the house in Verona
   supposedly inhabited by the model for
   Shakespeare's character Juliet, the
   walls of which are covered in declarations of love by fans of the legend of
   "Romeo and Juliet."

4 Parallel Lines chest of drawers
   James remade this Danish 1960s chest
   of drawers based on the Blondie album
   "Parallel Lines."

5 Genoa table
   An Italian table from the 1940s
   that has come under the influence
   of Mondrian.

1

KJELLGREN KAMINSKY ARCHITECTURE
Fredrik Kjellgren & Joakim Kaminsky
Pirate Baroque stackable seating
(opposite page)

KIK!
Kiki van Eijk
1   Modern Delft Tile Chair
Traditional Delft tile forms the basis for
a series of furniture, including a chaise-
longue and six stools that are adorned with
modern scenes. Instead of a sea battle,
the pattern depicts a mosque being bom-
bed by a B2 airplane. From a distance it
looks like a naive pattern but on approaching users discover images of modern-day
"hard" times on a soft "tile" instead of the
"soft" artistocratic scenes of the past on a
hard ceramic tile.

JANTZE BROGÅRD ASSHOFF
Noon furniture
2,3 Bench
4   Table
Inspired by traditional wood turned furniture, Swedish folklore and jewellery. A
set of table and bench with sustainable
solutions in mind, such as a construction
of Swedish Birch and a knock down construction for flat packaging.

3

2

4

PAUL LOEBACH

"I'm interested in the point at which something familiar becomes surprising," says Brooklyn-based furniture and product designer Paul Loebach who has become a master at combining old and new, traditional and experimental. "I think the form of my designs comes from my drive to push the limits of what a given material can do, and to challenge what we are conditioned to recognise as "normal."

Loebach's wooden Shelf Space was made in collaboration with an aerospace manufacturer who uses computer-controlled, multi-axis machining equipment to cut the wood away. Its liquid-looking form, which seems to flow off the wall and bank slightly before returning to it, pushes the limits of wood engineering and advanced machining technology. This is typical Loebach: the use of a traditional material and cutting-edge technology to generate an unlooked-for continuity between innovation and tradition.

Loebach grew up in the industrial Midwest of the United States and studied at the Rhode Island School of Design. Descended from a long line of German woodworkers, he learned the basics of the craft from a young age. His father, however, was a manufacturing engineer who developed new plastic forming technologies during the 1970s, so Loebach sees his work as a connection between the fresh technology and the enduring craft. "I work with a variety of materials but wood is my favourite starting point," Loebach says. "It's a material that already looks great before you do anything to it, so as a designer it's a simple matter of making sure you don't mess it up."

The designer's "neo-Roman" side table, Vase Space, has its roots in American Federal furniture and the West's obsession with classical forms. Three removable vases grow out of the tabletop, fabricated using a new multi-axis computer numerically controlled (CNC) technology.

"Design is a language," says Loebach. "Instead of words, the language of design uses shapes and materials to communicate a message. Our material world is therefore a structure of messages that tells the story of who we are." And who we could be.

1 **Vase Space**
Inspired by American Federal furniture and western society's obsession with classical form, this "neo-Roman" side table integrates three removable vases that visually flow into the table top. Machined using a new multi-axis CNC technology, this table is the result of a four-month experimental collaboration with an American aerospace manufacturer.

2 **Chair-O Space**
Inspired in equal parts by Chinese classicism and Roman antiquity, this chair replaces traditional hand-craftsmanship with computer-driven machinery that quickly articulates the contoured parts including traditional wood joinery. The chair's form evolved from a meticulous 3-D design process in collaboration with top engineers.

3 **Shelf Space**
This shelf's fluid form pushes the limits of wood engineering and advanced machining technology. This sweeping gesture employs traditional materials to invoke a dialog between technologically driven innovation and the continuity of historic reference.

1

3

2

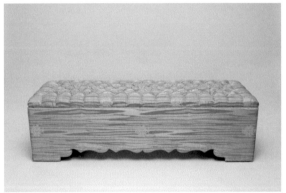

MINALE-MAEDA
Kuniko Maeda, Mario Minale
Survival furniture
1 Chandelier
2 Bench
3 Shelf
4 Table
5 Chair
6 Shelf and chandelier

This collection expresses the tension between the natural and the man-made as well as realism versus romanticism, pitting wood against woven fabric and the "good old times" of the past, expressed in the archetypical shapes, against contemporary daily life, expressed in the rough, simple construction. The elements of a period room are skilfully upholstered in silk brocade which has been dyed and woven using historical techniques by a manufacturer that dates back to the Industrial Revolution.

JANTZE BROGÅRD ASSHOFF
Pages 210–211, 251, 254

Stockholm-based Jantze Brogård Asshoff design furniture that isn't merely luxurious and playful; it draws its user into the decadence and the game. In 2008, founders Moa Jantze, Hanna Brogård and Johanna Asshoff played with the notion of listening at the keyhole, making the lacquered wood Cabinet, a cartoonish display case with huge keyhole cut-outs that serve as handles and through which one can either reveal or hide one's tableware.

Pairing modern with traditional, humble and high-end, handicraft with industrial production and whimsy with concern for the environment, while drawing on traditional Swedish folk costumes, JBA created a sofa defined by its detail, a series of chunky embroidered buttons. The peaked roof of their Greenhouse lacquered metal wastepaper basket opens to receive rubbish and comes in various sizes to make sorting one's trash (or recycling) a bit more entertaining. JBA's Noon bench and table are slimmed-down and simplified versions of traditional turned wood furniture but were also influenced by Swedish folklore and jewellery. Noon also has the virtue of its knock-down construction for flat pack shipping, reminding us that practical design never ever has to be dull.

1

1   Peek cupboard
    A modern display case in which you
    can choose to expose or hide your
    tableware. The generous keyholes also
    works as handles.

2   Greenhouse rubbish bin

2

WIS DESIGN
Anna Irinarchos

1 The Jewellery Lamp
Instead of letting jewellery get tangled on hooks or hidden in boxes Irinarchos brings them into the light. When your jewellry isn't adorning you, it can adorn the lamp.

MALIN LUNDMARK

2 Jewellery Lamp
A pendant lamp from which you can hang your favourite necklace.

3 Drawers in your Handbag

4 Jewellery drawer
With inspiration from intarsia, Lundmark has created a huge jewel box in the shape of a drawer.

ÜNAL BÖLER STUDIO
Alper Böler & Ömer Ünal

5 Kanca
Kanca means "hook" in Turkish and is a magazine holder that can double as multi-purpose hangers. Its form is reminiscent of the old forged metal door and window architectural fixtures in Istanbul.

DING3000
Carsten Schelling, Sven Rudolph,
Ralf Webermann
Animal Tales Collection
Ding3000 thought to themselves: "Mother
Nature is still the best designer in the
world" and began copying her most fasci-
nating creations, including floating Afghan
hounds, shy giraffes, greedy chicks and
not-at-all-stubborn mules.

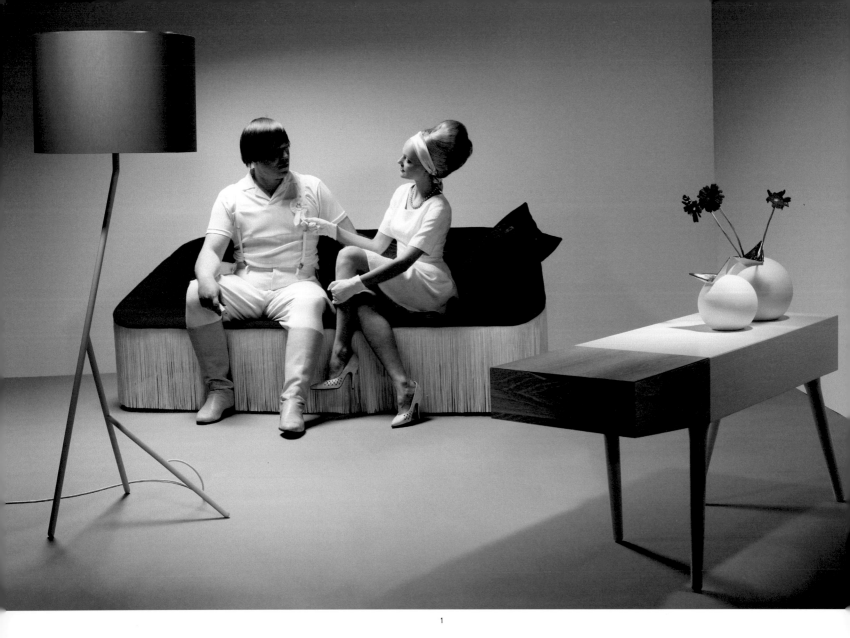

1

2

DING3000
Carsten Schelling, Sven Rudolph,
Ralf Webermann
1 Animal Tales Collection

2 Oderda table
An embedded joint in the edge of the
table top that can support any add-on
component, ranging from table legs
to a drawer or files. Each item can be
assigned to an individual position. Thus,
additional elements increase the table's
tidiness even though it appears less tidy.

DING3000
Carsten Schelling, Sven Rudolph,
Ralf Webermann

1 Cuco vase
This design is inspired by the image of
a hungry cuckoo chick.

2 Jirafa lamp
A standing lamp inspired by a giraffe.

3 Muli sideboard
A sideboard inspired by a mule.

4 Tazi sofa
A sofa inspired by an Afghan hound.

POSTFOSSIL
Pages 260–261

A 10-person Swiss design collective congealed around the question of humanity's post-fossil fuel future as Postfossil in 2007. Postfossil's first presentation at the 2008 Milan furniture fair offered 10 designs intended to heat up the debate about how to cope with a precipitously cooling relationship with our natural resources. The pieces remind us that the smallest efforts (even being willing to give the problem a little thought on a daily basis) can produce big results.

Anna Blattert and Daniel Gafner's chamfered steel and hand-blown glass First Light prototype is a retro-futuristic floor lamp powered, like clockworks, by a weight and cog wheels. No need to connect to a wall outlet; it generates its own electricity while users watch their very own power utility at work through the glass shade.

Christine Birkhoven's candleholder-shaped bedside lamp, Good Night Eileen, charges its low-energy LED on a flat charging station through magnetic induction and then glows for several minutes before fading, eliminating the need to switch lights on and off as one pads down the hall to kitchen or bath during the wee hours.

The sports furniture collection by Florian Hauswirth and Thomas Walde can be used to work out in – and handsomely furnish – the home. The pull-up bar doubles as a garment rack, the felt and leather stretching mat serves as a carpet and the bench can be used for doing sit ups. Best of all, the designers built the set to outlive its (admittedly healthy) user.

A gold pendant necklace by Anna Blattert and Claudia Heiniger holds a glass amulet filled with oil. Usually considered a valuable commodity only in the abstract (and often not considered much at all in the developed world), now that the West must pay dearly to fill gas tanks and transport tomatoes, this design may at last put crude oil – and human priorities – in their proper place.

1

2

3

Anna Blattert, Daniel Gafner

1 First Light
This reading lamp is powered through a weight and cog wheels just like clockworks. The power does not come from the socket but is produced directly in the body of the object. Through the glass lampshade the movement of the cog wheels is visible.

Die Seiner/Florian Hauswirth & Thomas Walde

2 Sports Furniture
The sports furniture collection is primarily intended to maintain physical fitness at home but is simultaneously a furniture collection that easily blends into the living space. The clothing rack is also a pull-up bar. The stretching mat serves as a carpet. The collection also includes a bench, skipping rope and cup.

Michael Niederberger

3 Branch Series
Branch Series is composed of connecting elements such as tree branches that bring nature indoors in the form of a table, chair, stool or coffee table. The series also includes a small candle attachment which throws bundled light onto the table through the aid of a parabolic reflector and a glass lens.

Corina Zuberbuehler

4,5 THESPILL bench
A reconfigurable seating element with integrated cushions, wall covering and rug that resemble an oil spill when put together.

Christine Birkhoven

6 Good Night Eileen lamp
Like an old-fashioned hand torch, this porcelain light allows users to avoid turning lights on and off as they move through a darkened house and is recharged on a charging base through magnetic induction.

4

5

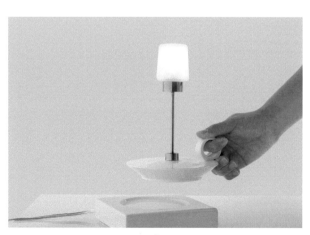

6

KATRIN SONNLEITNER

1 English Moving Habits installation
An installation that takes an experimental approach to the familiar by challenging the sequences of motion (and the expectations) that we are accustomed to with unconventional furniture modifications. In this interior, drawers open in odd directions or stay attached to the wall while only the frame moves forward. Furthermore, the drawer-like storage units offer innovative design solutions for domestic and work space, as well as for shopfittings.

PHILIPPE MALOUIN

2 Grace table
Malouin worked with Eurocraft, a leading manufacturer of inflatable structures to developed a grand table, big enough to accommodate 10 guests when inflated and small enough to fit in a duffel bag when deflated.

3 Hanger chair

4 Ballpoint stool
Malouin tracks a user's behaviour using furniture fitted with ball transfers like an oversized ballpoint pen. The final product is a transparent stool, its legs filled with ink, that can also track motion, write and draw.

1

3

2

4

DESIGN VIRUS
Pieke Bergmans & Peter Van Der Jagt
Melted Collection
From up close, the edges of these polystyrene foam shelves are deformed and
melted, indicating that they were in fact
baked to achieve their final forms.

VOW by HOW ABOUT VIKTOR
Yuki Abe, Helga Lahtinen,
Taina Lehtinen, Anna Salonen
& Marko Nenonen
Pages 265–266

VOW is an eclectic group of quirky furniture designed by Helsinki-based collective How About Viktor. Members Yuki Abe, Helga Lahtinen, Taina Lehtinen, Anna Salonen and Marko Nenonen produce interiors and products, as a group and independently.

Some pieces have metaphorical aspects to them. Abe's Atomos is a dynamic-looking candleholder with removable metal caps that allow it to be rotated and the number of candles altered, suggesting that atomic power doesn't hold a candle to candlepower. The name of Marko Nenonen's Campanula aluminum suspension lamp translates to "little bell" in Latin. Intended for use above the dining table, it is a symbol calling the family to gather for meals. Regardless of the type of energy-saving (and therefore usually cool in colour) bulb used, optional colours lining the inside of the shade give light a warm tone.

Other How About Viktor designs are intended simply to beautify the home or office and, at times, to multi-task in practical ways. Helga Lahtinen's Calvino bookshelf reveals preferred book covers and hides the rest. Kirin is a tall bar stool or chair that can also be used for hanging clothes. Abe's Maneki chair has limbs like a children's building block and features a diagonal arm that "waves its 'hand'" inviting one to sit, and tripling as a coat rack or a peg for a handbag or hat. Nenonen's Fold table is actually folded from thin sheet metal, using construction techniques borrowed from paper-folding, lending a slender structure strength and poetry.

Viktor On Wheels Collection 2008
Viktor on Wheels is a collection of furniture designed by How About Viktor – a Helsinki-based collective of five designers.

Marko Nenonen
1 Fold table
   Folded out of thin sheet metal, the legs
   of these tables create a superstructure
   to carry table tops without any additional constructions. Fold borrows construction techniques from paper-folding.

Yuki Abe
2 Kirin chair/garment rack
3 Maneki chair/coat hanger

4 Hanabi armchair
   This armchair is made of 12 modulated
   fabric bags filled with polystyrene
   pellets and can be used individually or
   combined with other Hanabis to form
   a sofa.

Marko Nenonen
5 Campanula pendant light

HOW ABOUT VIKTOR
Yuki Abe
Atomos candleholder
This modular candleholder that can be
rotated to any position.

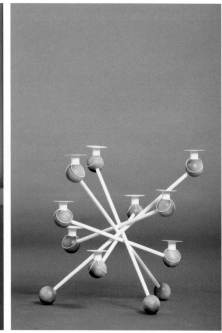

ROBERT STADLER
Light installation for Nuit Blanche Paris
Visitors entered the Saint-Paul Saint-Louis
church through a side door to find a scat-
tered group of luminous spheres hovering
above the choir. As one approached, the
cluster formed itself into a question mark.
As one passed through the church, however, the figure became abstracted again in
order to echo the figures of other hanging
lights dotting the cathedral. The question
(or doubt) is absorbed by the space.

TJEP.
Janneke Hooymans &
Frank Tjepkema
ROC Care furniture
Furniture for the reception area of the
Care & Health department of the ROC
professional training school in Apeldoorn,
the Netherlands. The idea of well-being
and care was manifest in different interior
elements. A protective shelter in the shape
of a large box forms a relaxation area.
Tidy made-up beds become chairs. Soft
mattresses form the reception desk. There
is a table protected by a tent that creates
an informal meeting space.

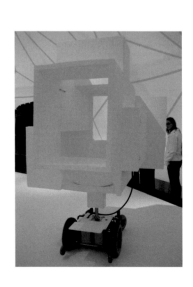

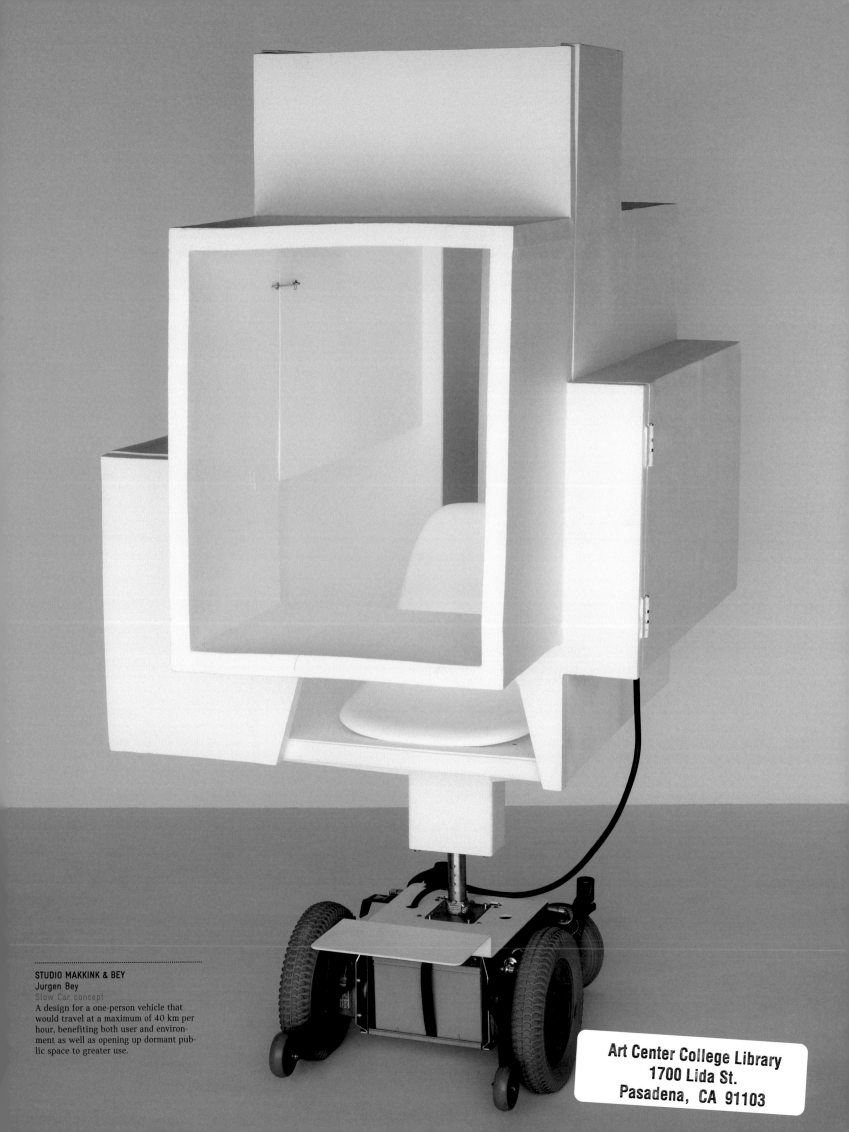

STUDIO MAKKINK & BEY
Jurgen Bey
Slow Car concept
A design for a one-person vehicle that would travel at a maximum of 40 km per hour, benefiting both user and environment as well as opening up dormant public space to greater use.

STUDIOILSE
Ilse Crawford
Pages 45, 270–274

Product design and interiors maven Ilse Crawford rose to prominence when she designed her modern take on turned wood. Her saucily titled 36-24-36 collection lacquers simple turned wood pieces in bright solid colors and pairs her spare burlesque (not an oxymoron, in this case) lamps with oversized shades to bring them into the 21st century. Taking the lathe-turned Victorian/Edwardian aesthetic to the nth degree, she has also produced a rug and fabrics for Christopher Farr using the shape as a graphical icon.

Crawford is the creative director and designer of studioilse and chairs the Department of Man and Well-Being at the Design Academy Eindhoven. She once served as the editor of BARE magazine and was founding editor of Elle Decor UK. During the 90s she developed the aesthetic for the exclusive Soho House franchise, mixing highly graphic wallpapers with classic Modernist furniture to create a retro-modernist gentleman's club for anyone, man or woman, with money. She also shone as creative director of one installment of the Swarovski Crystal Palace project, commissioning designers such as Hella Jongerius and Tom Dixon to remake the chandelier, and showing the resulting decadent pieces within the deteriorating walls of a disused factory.

Crawford's interiors translate her product design into similar environments and are often an eclectic synthesis that calls to mind both art and science. She will pare down more historical rococo elements while adding lean doses of ornament to the contemporary bits. In 2007, she restored the historic interior of Aesop's first stand-alone beauty product shop in the UK, exposing the original patina-ed parquet floors, fireplaces and high ceilings. Her design of two Mathias Dahlgren restaurants in the Grand Hotel Stockholm evoked a cleaner, idealised Industrial Age in the form of a train station-like atmosphere that features wood panelling, encaustic tile, cast iron and zinc. Crawford has a spot-on intuition about how to mix Carlo Scarpa with Studio Job, or Vico Magistretti with Josef Frank, and she executes it with a rare grace.

Wellcome Trust Club Room
To launch the new £30 million Wellcome collection, Studioilse designed interiors that are a fusion of art and science, from the books to the pictures and furniture. Crawford filled a room in the heart of the building a mixture of rational Prouve chairs with playful Castiglioni lights, improvised-looking Martino Gamper shelves and the beautifully engineered Eileen Grey one-armed non-conformist chairs.

STUDIOILSE
Ilse Crawford
Mathias Dahlgren restaurants
at Grand Hotel Stockholm

Studioilse used Mathias Dahlgren's food philosophy, combining local pride with a global perspective, as the springboard for her design of two of his restaurant interiors. In the Matbaren, the food bar, which is a quicker eating experience, and the Matsalen, the restaurant, they appealed to all the senses. They gave the Matbaren the atmosphere of a bustling train station, using robust materials such as wood panelling, encaustic tile and zinc. There are tables in wood and cast iron and raw Swedish primitive pieces from the 1700s, a mix of Scandinavian and international furniture.

Meanwhile, in the Matsalen, the atmosphere is more intimate and rarified, a place to linger instead of depart. Here they installed a parquet floor in Hungarian Point, Chesterfield sofas in velvet, and gilded metals, as well as salvaging many of the chairs from around the hotel and rehabilitating them in dyed yellow leather. Paired with chairs by Josef Frank from Svenskt Tenn are tables that have the burlesque bases designed by Studioilse. In the bar, the walls were painted a dark indigo to show off the historic floor and a golden screen from Studio Job.

STUDIOILSE
Ilse Crawford
Aesop shop, London
Aesop's first London shop is located in
a Victorian Grade II listed mansion block
on Mount street in Mayfair. Crawford's
design restored the historic interior, opened up the old fireplaces and exposed the
high ceilings but left the original parquet
floors raw with patination. The studio's
grand gesture, however, is a large ceramic
basin that anchors the centre of the interi-
or and emphasises the notion of cleansing.

STUDIO EDWARD VAN VLIET
Edward van Vliet
Nooon bar

Nooon is a comfortable and deluxe wine and food bar in the business district of south Amsterdam. Van Vliet looked to the East for inspiration, creating lasercut wall panels and a printed wallpaper. His palette consists of shades typical of India: fuschia pink, scarlet and a burnished gold. He upholstered low bespoke armchairs in pink velour and red fabric. The custom-made drum lamp shades feature a golden cage with a white screen-printed pattern on gold silk.

TJEP.
Pages 268, 276–277

That's Tjep. Full stop. And that small dot says a lot about this little product design studio. It's almost as if the studio has its own personality – and it is the personality of an extremely intelligent stand-up comedian.

It is no coincidence perhaps that the Amsterdam-based designers return again and again to the use of rubber, the material that is key to all comedy. In the process of designing their rubber-lined Shockproof vases, the pair threw vases off buildings, dropped vases from speeding cars, emptied a quiver of arrows into vases, hired a martial arts master to karate chop vases, shot one vase by Hella Jongerius with 10 bullets and cracked up two signed Egg vases donated to them for the purpose by Marcel Wanders. They also designed a sofa in the form of a nest made of giant rubber twigs.

Tjep. designers Frank Tjepkema and Janneke Hooymans met at the Eindhoven Design Academy in the 1990s. Today, they work with a wide range of materials and create everything from wallpaper, royal tiaras, corporate identities and interiors to mobile phones and cracked rubber vases (if only they could make the phones as durable). In 2008, a restaurant called Praq commissioned Tjep. to design an interior for their Amersfoort eatery that would welcome families without looking like a child's sandbox. Beneath a massive, wood-beamed roof, they constructed furniture that multitasked. For instance, a table becomes a window or a bus or kitchen, while anchoring the centre of the room is a wall that looks like a sherbet-coloured game of Connect Four. A little amuse-bouche for the adults, a little amusement for the kids. Tjep. seem to be searching for beauty, meaning – and always a bit of fun – in places where it is assumed that none exists. And they keep finding it.

Praq Amersfoort restaurant
Tjep. was commissioned by Praq to design two eateries that would appeal to both adults and children. The first of the two opened in Amersfoort, the Netherlands and is dominated by a monumental roof composed of massive wooden beams. Beneath it some furniture playfully performs more than one task. For example, a table becomes a window, a bus and a kitchen. A six-metre-high partition in the center of the restaurant looks like a colourful game while complimenting the rustic-modern architecture.

1

2

3

1 The bar at Karriere Bar, Copenhagen
Located in the Flæsketorvet neighbour-
hood in Copenhagen, Karriere Bar was
not designed by one person; instead it
incorporates pieces by world-class designers and artists who work in a range
of disciplines and whose contributions
have defined the operations and am-
bience of the space.

MASSIMO BARTOLINI
2   Fountain perfumed water installation

OLAFUR ELIASSON
3   National Career lamp

DAN GRAHAM
4   Dividing Wall

BANK & RAU
4   Meat and Tool benches and tables

ERNESTO NETO
5   Aaaaaaaaaaaaaa!!! lounge furniture

FRANZ ACKERMANN
6   Wall Painting

4

5

6

As blunt as a declaration of war and as piercing as beauty can be, it is an announcement of times to come. The Femme et la Maison collection is, first and foremost, turning the last sighs of the patriarchy into the cries of the she-almighty. Her shyness has now been replaced with the naked curves and shapes of lust and desire. Her passivity has been succeeded by the skilfully masked determination to rule your home. Nika Zupanc upgrades her previous collection of purposefully and emotionally destabilized projects with yet another assortment of charming collectables." Text by Igor Medjugorac

Page 229: Lolita Polycarbonate, Pll • **Producer:** Moooi • **Photo Credit:** Maarten Van Houten

O-D-A (OBJECT DESIGN ALLIANCE)
Jutamas Buranajade + Piti Amraranga
(Thailand)
www.o-d-a.net
Pages 16, 87

Page 16: Taste of Tea Wood • **Client/Label:** nextmaruni • **Photo Credit:** Yoneo Kawabe for nextmaruni • **Comments:** Grand Prix winner of Wooden Armchairs Competition by nextmaruni (judged by product designer, Jasper Morrison)
Page 16: NRML Wood • **Client:** Promosedia • **Edition:** Prototype • **Photo Credit:** Promosedia
Page 87: Sub-Stool Aluminum sheet • **Producer:** restrogen

OD-V (Netherlands)
Onno Donkers
www.od-v.nl
Pages 152, 160, 166

Page 152: Little Strong Chair New and old wood • **Edition:** on demand
Page 160: Pallet-Bar Wood, adjustable legs, bolts, pipe, aluminium sheet • **Client:** Bonanza Coffee Heroes Berlin • **Edition:** Unique
Page 160: Legs Wood, screws, paint • **Client:** Bonanza Coffee Heroes Berlin • **Edition:** Unique • **Photo Credit:** Kiduk Reus
Page 160: Crate-Top MDF, high-gloss paint • **Client:** Bonanza Coffee Heroes Berlin • **Edition:** On demand • **Photo Credit:** Kiduk Reus
Page 160: Branch-Table Wood • **Edition:** Unique
Page 160: Aluminium Table Aluminium, desktop, bolts • **Client:** Bonanza Coffee Heroes Berlin • **Edition:** On demand • **Photo Credits:** Kiduk Reus
Page 166: Trojan Horse Wood, screws, glass • **Client:** Van Abbe Museum, Eindhoven • **Edition:** Unique • **Photo Credit:** Onno Donkers
Page 166: Shower Tents bath-tubs, wood, plastic, plumber-materials • **Edition:** Unique • **Comments:** The bathing-units were especially made for "Nuits Blanches"; a temporary hotel during the international filmfestival in Rotterdam.

OLAFUR ELIASSON (Iceland)
www.karrierebar.com
Page 278

Page 278: National Career • **Client:** Karrierebar • **Photo Credits:** Anders Sune Berg

OSKAR ZIETA (Poland, Switzerland)
www.zieta.pl
Pages 87, 120–121

Pages 87, 120–121: The Lamp/The Chair Plopp/The Stool Plopp/Prototype Sheet metal • **Edition:** Prototype for limited edition
Page 120: Aufgeblasene Designer Sheet metal • **Comments:** Supervision: Oskar Zieta Participating students: Abel Blancas Moran, Ferdinand Carl Facklam, Tariq Gardizi, Seong Ki Lee, Georg Anton Munkel, Varuna Saini, Alexandra Stamou

Page 121: The Stool Plopp Polished sheet metal • **Client:** hay.dk • **Edition:** Limited

OSKO + DEICHMANN (Germany)
www.oskodeichmann.com
Pages 25–26

Page 25: Clip Chair Solid beech or wenge frame, lacquered in white RAL • **Producer:** Moooi
Page 26: Pebble Steel frame, foam, fabric • **Client:** Elmar Flötotto

OVERTREDERS W (Netherlands)
Reinder Bakker/Hester van Dijk
www.overtreders-w.nl
Page 159

Page 159: Karavaan Festivalwood, straps • **Producer:** Psychiatric institution in Heiloo, one of the sources of the festivalwood, straps • **Photo Credit:** Reinder Bakker

PATRICIA URQUIOLA (Italy)
www.patriciaurquiola.com
Pages 24, 78–79, 85, 102–103

Page 24: Bohemien • **Producer:** Moroso
Page 78: RE-TROUVÉ Metal • **Producer:** Emu • **Photo Credit:** Studiopiù Communication S.r.l.
Page 79: Tropicalia • **Producer:** Moroso
Pages 85, 102–103: Antibodi • **Producer:** Moroso

PATRICK GAVIN (United States)
www.pgavin.com
Pages 50–51

Page 50: Room Divider Powder-coated aluminium, black walnut wood • **Edition:** Limited • **Photo Credit:** Patrick Gavin
Page 51: Basic Boundaries Upholstered Screen with Zipper, Stainless Steel Rod, Powder-coated Steel, Polished Aluminum • **Edition:** Limited

PATRICK NORGUET (France)
www.patricknorguet.com
Pages 24, 26, 40–41, 43, 58–59

Page 24: Lex/
Page 26: Whats/
Page 43: Lila/
Page 59: Looks/Apollo • **Client:** Artifort
Page 40: Spirit/Silvera Collection 01/Nao/Folio Metal • **Client:** Silvera
Page 41: Element • **Client:** Artoria
Pages 58–59: F117 • **Client:** Thonet Vienna
Page 58: Boson
Page 59: E • **Client:** Harvink

PAUL LOEBACH (United States)
www.paulloebach.com
Pages 99, 252

Page 99: Step Stools Hard maple, birch plywood • **Photo Credit:** Jeremy Frechette
Page 252: Vase Space/Chair-O Space/Shelf Space Hard maple wood/wool upholstery/basswood • **Photo Credit:** Jeremy Frechette

PEPE HEYKOOP (Netherlands)
www.pepeheykoop.nl
Pages 200, 266

Page 200: Tape-Pot Ceramic, glaze

Page 266: Conversations Various second-hand lamps, fabric • **Edition:** Prototypes for limited editions

PER EMANUELSSON & BASTIAN BISCHOFF (Sweden)
www.perandbastian.com
Page 206

Page 206: Surveillancelight 2008 Aluminium, metal • **Photo Credits:** Chris Knox

PETER MARIGOLD (United Kingdom)
www.petermarigold.com
Page 167

Page 167: Tilt Series Beech and utility plywood • **Client:** Paul Smith • **Edition:** Eight existing currently • **Comments:** The units were created specifically to display clothing and accessories, which distinguishes them from normal bookshelves.

PETER BRANDT (Sweden)
www.blastation.se
Page 49

Page 49: Bimbo Compression-moulded birch veneer • **Producer:** Blå Station • **Photo Credit:** Erik Karlsson

PHIL CUTTANCE (New Zealand)
www.philcuttance.com
Page 248

Page 248: Fantasy Fantasy Inkjet-printed fabric, foam, pine frame • **Edition:** Limited • **Comments:** The chair breaks down into a seat, back and a pair of arms, easily assembled with connector bolts.

PHILIP EDIS (Sweden)
www.philipedis.com
Pages 29, 41, 248

Page 29: Authority System Milled MDF • **Photo Credit:** Louise Billgert
Page 41: Twist Steel, wood • **Producer:** Design House Stockholm • **Photo Credit:** Mikael Ek.
Page 248: Let Loose Wood, textile • **Photo Credit:** Fredrik Sandin Carlson

PHILIP MICHAEL WOLFSON
(United Kingdom)
www.wolfsondesign.com
Pages 86, 93

Page 86: Longevity Zitan wood • **Producer:** Contrasts Gallery • **Edition:** Limited to five • **Photo Credits:** Contrasts gallery • **Comments:** 74 × 180 × 110 cm
Page 93: LineDesk Painted, bent and welded aluminium • **Producer:** Patrick Brillet Fine Art • **Edition:** Limited edition of 10 • **Photo Credit:** Maxim Nilov • **Comments:** Available through Patrick Brillet Fine Art

PHILIPPE MALOUIN (United Kingdom)
www.philippemalouin.com
Page 262

Page 262: Hanger Chair Marine rubber, steel, birch • **Photo Credit:** Rene van der Hulst • **Comments:** This chair is available at Spazio Rosanna Orlandi in Milan, Gallery Fumi in London and at Sid-Lee in Amsterdam, as well as Commissaires in Montreal.
Page 262: Grace Marine rubber, steel, rope, birch • **Producer:** Self-produced in collaboration with Eurocraft • **Edition:** Limited • **Photo Credit:** Rene van der Hulst • **Comments:** The table is available at Gallery Fumi in London, Rossana Orlandi in Milan and Moss

Gallery in New York and Los Angeles.
Page 262: Ballpoint PMMA, polyester resin, stainless steel casters, oil-based ink • **Edition:** Limited

PLATFORM STUDIO (Belgium)
Jan Wertel & Gernot Oberfell
www.materialise-mgx.com
Page 134

Page 134: Fractal-T Epoxy • **Producer:** Materialise.MGX • **Edition:** Unique • **Photo Credits:** Platform Studio with Matthias Bär

POSTFOSSIL (Switzerland)
www.postfossil.ch
Pages 260–261

Page 260: First Light Chamfered steel, hand-blown glass • **Edition:** Prototype • **Photo Credit:** Anna Blattert
Page 260: Sports Furniture Oak, ash, leather, glass and metal • **Label:** Postfossil • **Photo Credit:** Christian Senti
Page 260: Branch Series aluminium cast parts, branches, wooden board • **Photo Credit:** Chrisitan Senti
Page 261: Good Night Eileen Porcelain, glass, stainless steel • **Label:** Postfossil • **Photo Credits:** Christian Senti
Page 261: THESPILL Cardboard, cellular material, polyurethane • **Edition:** Prototype • **Photo Credit:** Christian Senti

R&SIE (Belgium)
François Roche
www.materialise-mgx.com
Page 135

Page 135: I've Heard About Polyamide • **Producer:** Materialise.MGX • **Edition:** Unique

RAINER SPEHL (Germany)
www.rainerspehl.com
Page 31

Page 31: The New Konk Oak and ash timber, clear and smoked glass, nickel plated steel tube, various other aterials • **Client:** KonK • **Edition:** On-off • **Photo Credit:** Achim Hatzius
Page 31: Hanging Closet Pitch pine • **Edition:** Unique

RAPHAEL VON ALLMEN (Switzerland)
www.raphaelvonallmen.com
Pages 14, 68, 99

Pages 14, 68: Plastic Back Chair Polypropylene, aluminium • **Edition:** Prototype • **Photo Credits:** (black) ECAL/Florian Joye (beige) ECAL/Raphaël von Allmen
Page 99: Gum Tab Synthetic gum, PUR binder, steel • **Edition:** Prototype

RAW-EDGES (United Kingdom)
Shay Alkalay & Yael Mer
www.raw-edges.com
Page 98

Page 98: Stack Wood • **Producer:** Established & Sons • **Photo Credits:** (3) Mike Goldwater
Page 98: Pivot Lacquered wood, solid oak, solid American walnut • **Client/Producer:** Arco • **Photo Credit:** Petrik Pantze

READYMADE PROJECTS (United States)
Stephen Burks
www.readymadeprojects.com
Pages 85, 100–101, 213

TAKASHI SATO (Japan)
www.takashisato.jp
Pages 39, 47, 57, 69

Page 39: Coat Hanger Beech, aluminium • Comments: Nominated for Design Report Award 2008.
Page 47: Tongs Aluminium • Comments: Tongs was exhibited at the SaloneSatellite 2008.
Page 57: Kaki Glass, ceramic • Comments: Kaki was exhibited at the Stockholm Furniture Fair 2007.
Page 69: Pata Felt, plywood • Comments: Pata was exhibited in Stockholm Furniture Fair, 2007, and SaloneSatellite 2008.

TAKESHI MIYAKAWA (USA)
www.tmiyakawadesign.com
Pages 32, 97

Page 32: Fractal 23 Oil-painted plywood
Page 97: Wedge Table Oil-painted plywood
Page 97: 3x3 Chair Stained plywood

TARO & SARAH (Germany)
www.taroandsarah.com
Page 173

Page 173: My Cloud Body: polystyrene/white satinized light source: High-power LED magnetic connection points work as connectors and power supply

THOMAS FEICHTNER/BUCHEGGER, DENOTH, FEICHTNER (Austria)
Thomas Feichtner
www.bdf-id.com
Pages 84, 90–92, 95

Pages 84, 92: Axiome Aluminium, powder coated • Producer: Designwerkstaette Schatzl, Austria
Page 90: Water Bottle Green glass • Edition: Prototype
Page 90: Toplesschair Leather, chrome • Edition: Prototype fo limited edition
Page 90: Table Chair Leather, chrome, piano lacquer • Producer: Neue Wiener Werkstaetten, Austria
Page 90: Public Granulated foam plastic • Edition: Limited
Page 90: FSB 5930 Aluminium • Producer: FSB, Germany
Page 90: Eyry Lamp wireframe, tricot fabric • Edition: Limited/Prototype
Page 90: Cutt Silver 940/000 • Client/Producer: Wiener Silberschmiede Werkstaette, Austria
Page 90: Bric crystal • Edition: one off piece/prototype
Page 91: Honey Chair wood • Client/Producer: Holzwerkstatt Rehberger, Austria
Page 91: FX10 Lounge Chair wood, leather • Client/Producer: Neue Wiener Werkstaetten, Austria
Page 91: Coma aluminium, sheet metal Edition: Limited/Prototype
Page 95: Two Axiome in Rotation hand blown crystal • Client/Producer: J&L Lobmeyr, Austria

TJEP. (Netherlands)
Janneke Hooymans & Frank Tjepkema
www.tjep.com
Pages 268, 276–277

Page 268: ROC Care • Client: ROC Care • Producer: Iris • Photo Credits: Jannes Linders • Comments: Creative consultancy: Kunst en Bedrijf worked as creative consultancy in the selection of designers for the different departments, including: Jurgen Bey, Krijn de Kooning, Tejo Remy and Rene Veenhuizen.
Pages 276–277: Praq Amersfoort • Client: Praq Amersfoort • Comments: Project team Frank Tjepkema, Janneke Hooymans, Tina Stieger, Leonie Janssen, Bertrand Gravier, Camille Cortet

TOM DIXON (United Kingdom)
www.tomdixon.net
Pages 15, 18, 23, 240

Page 18: slab table and chairs oak
Page 15, 23: Mirror Balls on stand • Comments: Industrial strength heritage. Inspired by the lunar landing space helmets, the lamp is fashioned from high impact resistant polycarbonate normally used in bullet proofing and anti-vandal applications, making it almost indestructible.
Page 23: Cone lights Aluminium
Page 240: Fat spot Copper
Page 240: CU29 Copper

TOM PRICE (United Kingdom)
www.tom-price.com
Pages 82, 132

Pages 82, 132: Meltdown Chair Polypropylene tube PP Tube: • Edition: Limited to 12
Page 132: Meltdown Chair: PVC Hose PVC Hose • Edition: Limited to 12

TOMITA KAZUHIKO (Italy)
www.tomitadesign.com
Page 112

Page 112: Banana • Client: ARCADE
Page 112: Sususu • Client: VITTORIO BONACINA

TORD BOONTJE (France)
www.tordboontje.com
Pages 142, 162–163

Pages 142, 162–163: Witches' Kitchen Wood/Creamic • Producer: Artecnica • Photo Credits: Angela Moore

TRANLOGUE ASSOCIATES INC. (Japan)
www.tranlogue.jp/airLUCE
Page 243

Page 243: airLUCE • Client: Tranlogue Associates Inc. • Label: airLUCE by tranlogue associates • Producer: Motohiro Sugita • Comments: Surface-emitting acrylic board

ÜNAL & BÖLER STUDIO (Turkey)
Alper Böler, Ömer Ünal
www.unalboler.com
Pages 19, 79, 255

Page 19: Kase Oak, steel • Client: Cankat Clinic • Photo Credit: Tunc Suerdas
Page 79: Yosun Steel, PVC brushes, fabric lampshade • Edition: Prototype • Photo Credit: Ömer Ünal
Page 255: Kanca Steel, concrete • Client: Lush Hotel/Istanbul • Label: Kanca • Edition: Prototype • Photo Credit: Tunc Suerdas

VIABLE LONDON (United Kingdom)
www.viablelondon.com
www.decodelondon.com
Page 35, 79

Page 35: Selflife White or charcoal grey lacquered MDF • Producer: Decode London
Page 79: Wire Pendant Powder-coated or copper-plated steel wire • Producer: Decode London

VINTA (Japan)
Kohei Okamoto & Toshitaka Nakamura
www.vinta.jp
Page 207

Page 207: AfterDark ABS, steel pipe, 40W (100V) light bulb • Comments: Created for "Chocolate" exhibition at 21_21DESIGN SIGHT, Tokyo, 2007

VOONWONG & BENSONSAW (United Kingdom)
www.voon-benson.com
www.decodelondon.com
Pages 47, 81

Page 47: Slicebox Semi-matte or high-gloss lacquer • Producer: Decode London
Page 81: Tripod Black, white or stainless steel • Producer: Decode London

WANNES ROYAARDS (Netherlands)
www.royaardsenfontijn.nl
Page 207

Page 207: Bedside Table High-gloss aluminium, birch multiplex • Client: Lloyd Hotel Amsterdam • Producer: Royaards & Fontijn

WIS DESIGN (Sweden)
Lisa Widén & Anna Irinarchos
www.wisdesign.se
Pages 155, 206–207, 211, 255

Page 155: Decades
Page 206: Dot Painted aluminium, painted metal pipes, necklace/dimmer made of Swarovski pearls • Client/Producer: Lampister • Photo Credit: Lampister
Page 207: Proper Painted metal, brass net • Client/Producer: Rydéns/Smålandsdesign • Photo Credit: Niklas Palmklint
Page 211: Twine Painted MDF and painted steel wire • Producer: Casamania • Photo Credit: Henrik Bonnevier
Page 211: Camp Site Berns • Photo Credit: Henrik Bonnevier • Comments: This was a design exhibit at Stockholm Design Week during February 2008.
Page 255: The Jewellery Lamp Painted metal • Edition: Limited to 80 • Photo Credit: Anna Irinarchos • Comments: Not in production at the moment.

WOKMEDIA (China/United Kingdom)
Julie Mathias and Wolfgang Kaeppner
www.wokmedia.com
Pages 164, 185

DESIRE

THE SHAPE OF THINGS TO COME

Edited by Robert Klanten, Sven Ehmann,
Andrej Kupetz, Shonquis Moreno & Adeline Mollard

"About Desire", "Designing Desire", "The Economy of Desire"
& Chapter Introductions by Andrej Kupetz
Designer Profiles by Shonquis Moreno

Cover Motif: Studio Job/Job Smeets & Nynke Tynagel, "Collection FARM"
Cover Picture by Robert Kot, Brussels
Cover & Layout by Adeline Mollard for Gestalten
Typefaces: Catalog by Michael Mischler & Nik Thoenen
Foundry: www.binnenland.ch
Gravur Condensed by Cornel Windlin
Foundry: www.lineto.com

Project Management by Elisabeth Honerla for Gestalten
Production Management by Vinzenz Geppert for Gestalten
Proofreading by GlobalSprachTeam
Printed by fgb, Freiburg
Made in Germany

Published by Gestalten, Berlin 2008
ISBN 978-3-89955-218-8

Bibliographic information published by the Deutsche Nationalbibliothek.
The Deutsche Nationalbibliothek lists this publication in the Deutsche Nationalbibliografie;
detailed bibliographic data is available on the internet at http://dnb.d-nb.de.

None of the content in this book was published in exchange for payment by commercial parties or
designers; Gestalten selected all included work based solely on its artistic merit.

This book was printed according to the internationally accepted FSC standards for environmental
protection, which specify requirements for an environmental management system.

Gestalten is a climate neutral company and so are our products. We collaborate with the non-profit
carbon offset provider myclimate (www.myclimate.org) to neutralize the company's carbon footprint
produced through our worldwide business activities by investing in projects that reduce CO_2 emissions
(www.gestalten.com/myclimate).